A NOTE ON LITERARY CRITICISM

Books by James T. Farrell

STUDS LONIGAN

A Trilogy, comprising

YOUNG LONIGAN · THE YOUNG MANHOOD OF STUDS
LONIGAN · JUDGMENT DAY

GAS-HOUSE McGINTY

CALICO SHOES

GUILLOTINE PARTY

A Note on Literary Criticism

BY JAMES T. FARRELL

THE VANGUARD PRESS : NEW YORK

Foreword

In this book I make no pretense of being definitive, for in the field of criticism I can best describe myself as an amateur; in no sense do I consider myself a professional critic, let alone a professional Marxist.

I aim principally to open a critical discussion which will touch upon fundamental problems of literature and of criticism—their relation to each other and to the times in which we live. If this much is achieved, I shall be more than satisfied.

James T. Farrell

New York City.
March 10, 1936.

Contents

A NOTE ON LITERARY CRITICISM

CHAPTER I

The Duality of Literature

I THINK that literature must be viewed both as a branch of the fine arts and as an instrument of social influence. It is this duality, intrinsic to literature, that produces unresolved problems of literary criticism.

In order to analyze these problems, certain general conceptions must be presented. For purposes of intellectual convenience, I believe that we may divide human experience into two generalized categories: the æsthetic and the functional, the subjective and the objective. The æsthetic or subjective aspect of human experience deals with the pleasure, value, and elations which we derive from things, from qualities, and from intellectual, emotional, and physiological states as ends in themselves. The functional or objective aspect of experience deals with objects and actions in terms of their use-value. Thus, the functional or objective aspect of experi-

ence deals with objects and actions in terms of their
relatedness with other objects and actions. The æsthetic or subjective aspect refers to objects and
actions in their isolation or selection from other
objects and actions. Functional or objective activity, in terms of these categories, deals with serial
processes, and in these processes we look upon any
stage or sequence of the process only as it leads to
the next stage and thereby permits us to proceed
further toward concluding the process.[1]

I must say parenthetically that I have used the
phrase *aspects of experience* because I do not seek
to establish my categories as absolutes. One or the
other, the functional or the æsthetic, is given more
emphasis because of particular purposes, situations,
and necessities; moreover, when experience is har-

[1] This distinction is suggested and largely paraphrased from an article by
the late George Herbert Mead. "The Nature of an Æsthetic Experience,"
in *The International Journal of Ethics*, July, 1926. I have thus far only
glanced through John Dewey's *Art as Experience*, but this hasty reading,
plus my familiarity with Dr. Dewey's previous writings—particularly
Experience and Nature—suggests to me that he establishes a similar kind
of distinction. In fact, the Mead article was admittedly inspired by *Experience and Nature*. On page 15 of *Art as Experience* (Minton-Balch)
Dewey writes: "The difference between the esthetic and the intellectual is
thus one of the places where emphasis falls in the constant rhythm that
marks the interaction of the live creature with his surroundings. The
ultimate matter of both emphases in experience is the same." This is the
same distinction that I am making. Another reference here is a book
titled *Æsthetic Judgment*, by D. W. Prall (Crowell). It is about as complete a treatment of the subject from the pragmatic viewpoint as one can
get.

monious and coördinated, there is no split between the functional or objective and the æsthetic or subjective. Any complete divorcement of categories here leads to the vice of oversimplification; and unfortunately, both in the practice and in the theory of æsthetics and literary criticism, there have been glaring instances of such a divorcement.

CHAPTER II

Impressionism

THE divorcement or isolation of the æsthetic or
subjective category leads to pure æstheticism, a
philosophy of hedonism, a theory of art for art's
sake, or a method that is completely expressionistic
in literature, and impressionistic or sensationalistic
in criticism. A beautiful as well as famous description of such a divorcement on the æsthetic side is
to be found in Pater's conclusion to *The Renaissance*:

"To regard all things and principles of things as
inconstant modes or fashions has more and more
become the tendency of modern thought. . . .
The service of philosophy, of speculative culture
toward the human spirit, is to rouse, to startle it to
a life of constant and eager observation. Every
moment some form grows perfect in hand or face;
some tone on the hills or the sea is choicer than the
rest; some mood of passion or insight or intellectual

excitement is irresistibly real and attractive to us,—
for that moment only. Not the fruit of experience,
but experience itself, is the end. A counted number
of pulses only is given to us of a variegated, dramatic life. How may we see in them all that is to
be seen in them by the finest senses?" For with
"each mind keeping as a solitary prisoner its own
dream of a world," the ideal is "to burn always"
with "a hard, gem-like flame," and "only be sure it
is passion, . . . that it does yield you . . . fruit
of a quickened, multiplied consciousness. Of such
wisdom, the poetic passion, the desire of beauty, the
love of art for its own sake, has most. For art comes
to you proposing frankly to give nothing but the
highest quality to your moments as they pass, and
simply for those moments' sake."

Such an attitude leads to sensationalism and a
philosophy of novelty. It views art only as a means
of producing sensations in the audience. Objects
are perceived only for their own sake, and in dis-
relation from the process of which they are a part.
The past and the future of the æsthetic object tend
to become totally meaningless, for it is not the fruit
of experience and the experience itself that are emphasized, but solely the latter. The end result of
such a view is the formal exclusion of the functional or objective. This theory, consistently

adopted and utilized, leads to preciousness; and preciousness leads to sapped vitality, and then to surfeit.

Generally speaking, æsthetic experiences are a by-product of functional activities; and, similarly, the art of a society tends to be the by-product of the functioning of that society. Hence happiness and pleasure are usually the by-products of action and living. A sensationalistic æsthetic like Pater's removes the ends of pleasure and æsthetic appreciation from the stream of functioning, and absolutizes them; it turns the relationship between the æsthetic and the functional upside down. Happiness and pleasure are the ends; and living and functioning become the means to happiness and pleasure. Applied in criticism, the critic must, if he be consistent, hold merely to a recording of sensationalistic impressions; he must emphasize literature as pleasure, as the producing of quickened sensibilities and extended consciousness. He does not need to (in terms of this view) relate these results of literature into the area of social values.

An American apostle of impressionism whose writings have actually argued for a divorcement of æsthetics from the functional is Joel Elias Spingarn. In *Creative Criticism and Other Essays* (Harcourt, Brace and Company) he writes:

"To have sensations in the presence of a work of art and to express them, that is the function of Criticism for the impressionistic critic. His attitude he would express . . . : 'To read is for me to experience a thrill of pleasure. My delight . . . is itself a judgment, and what better judgment is it possible for me to give? All that I can do is to tell how it affects me, what sensations it gives me. . . . Each of us, if we are sensitive to impressions and express ourselves well, will produce a new work of art to replace the work which gives us our sensations. This is the art of Criticism, and beyond that Criticism cannot go.' . . . It is not the inherent function of poetry to further any moral or social cause, any more than it is the function of bridge-building to further the cause of Esperanto."

This mechanical theory performs the operation of separating art from all other spheres of interest. Thus Mr. Spingarn also says that if one deals with the biography and social backgrounds of a poet, one is no longer writing criticism, but history or sociology. This dictum locks out functions and separates them, thus breaking up the relationship of art with other aspects of the social process. It likewise removes criticism from its position in a larger social process, and art is thus viewed as the means for the reception of sensations alone. The logical result is that content becomes irrelevant or

17

incidental, and the artist is merely to be true to his vision, whatever that vision be. The critic is then to sense that vision, and build, on top of it, a new vision, creating a new work of art. The natural history of art and of æsthetic standards is ignored; concern with the content of art, and the social values that may be implicit or explicit in art, is delegated as a special extra-critical assignment.

Specific illustration can perhaps serve as the best refutation of such theories as that of Spingarn. For this purpose I shall take one of Santayana's finest sonnets from *Poems* (Scribner's):

> Though utter death should swallow up my hope
> And choke with dust the mouth of my desire,
> Though no dawn burst, and no aurorean choir
> Sing *Gloria Deo* when the heavens ope,
> Yet have I light of love, nor need to grope
> Lost, wholly lost, without an inward fire;
> The flame that quickeneth the world entire
> Leaps in my breast, with cruel death to cope.
> Hath not the night-environed earth her flowers?
> Hath not my grief the blessèd joy of thee?
> Is not the comfort of these singing hours,
> Full of thy perfectness, enough for me?
> They are not evil, then, those hidden powers:
> One love sufficeth an eternity.

A critical interpretation of this poem demands

18

an initial challenge of Mr. Spingarn's use of the word *vision*. For if we ask ourselves whether Santayana has been true to his vision, and what his vision is, we discover that we are not using the correct term. If we desire to keep our verbal coinage sound, we have to acknowledge that *vision* does not properly connote the content of the poem. For this sonnet is built on the basis of intellectual concepts. It opens by expressing doubt of the possibility of immortality. The poet says that even though there be no immortality, he can, if he have "light of love," be released from the need to grope, "lost, wholly lost, without an inward fire." For this possession gives him a flame that permits him to cope with the dark apprehensions of death. It provides justification for æsthetic moments that contain their own perfection. And, because of this, such a perfection is enough to suffice for an eternity.

To understand this poem, then, we must realize that it is not merely the presentation of a vision, but also is constructed from concepts. It expresses scepticism of an after-life and views the world and the interests of man within a naturalistic framework. It places a very significant value on the moment of æsthetic experience. Finally—if we give "light of love" a broad rather than a narrow meaning—we can interpret the poem as the passionate pursuit of an interest which makes possible a perfection of æsthetic experience, thereby knitting together functional and æsthetic purposes.

If we follow Mr. Springarn's dictum we must here pause and ask ourselves whether we are, or are not, practising the art of criticism. Does this poem, granting my analysis, produce only a sensation? Or does it represent a point of view, presenting intellectual concepts eloquently expressed in poetic form? Are we merely to say that it is Santayana's vision, that he has been true to it, and that it has stimulated in us another vision which we can describe? Or are we also to consider whether it expresses any truth? Have we no right to accept or to question the intellectual concepts out of which the poem is built? And is such an acceptance or rejection merely the expression of a new vision?

Suppose, for instance, a Spiritualist reads this poem, and understands it as a negation of immortality. On top of the poet's vision, he will build a vision of his own, describing how he expects, after death, to experience a perpetual perfection of singing hours in the third zone of the Summerland. And suppose I express a judgment of the poem, rationally stating why I think that the poem expresses a truth. Is the Spiritualist then practising the art of criticism? And am I, instead of holding

20

myself within the bounds of criticism, encroaching upon the precincts of philosophy? In other words, is criticism solely and fundamentally the registration of impressions, *sans* judgment? If so, Spingarn forces us either to reject the element of thought in criticism, or else to debase our coinage of words by neglecting to make any distinction between thought and sensation. All impressions upon us are, in his terms, reduced to the same category and level. And hence his critical dicta present the contention that criticism is not criticism, if it is judgment. And therefore, as a critical theorist, all that his formulation allows us to do with Santayana's sonnet is to state the terms of its "vision," and then to express our own vision in the creation of a new work of art. In other words, it is totally irrelevant for us to argue that the concepts out of which the poem is constructed are true, or are untrue. That would be philosophy. The soundness or unsoundness of the ideas in a work of literature is unimportant; only sensations and visions are to have a position in the art of criticism.

This analysis should suggest that any such theory is narrowing. The philosophy of art for art's sake must necessarily be the creed of a small aristocracy of æsthetes, since it detaches itself from everything except a limited sphere of artistic interests. As these interests are fostered, they become more and more removed from life; they lead toward a constantly increasing emphasis on perfection. This perfectionism does not grow out of the functioning of various social processes, including literature; hence the processes tend to get more removed from life. In other words, the art-for-art's-sake theory separates social processes by putting up fences around certain spheres of interest, or around the categories that suggest these spheres of interest. Particularly in times like the present, we can understand why this theory has earned unpopularity for itself. We must add, however, that this unpopularity and the words used to connote the theory have been carried to unnecessary extremes. The result of this extremism is a slurring over or ignoring of the real problem of æsthetics; with this slurring over, there has resulted in criticism a tendency toward the lessening of æsthetic sensibilities. It is consequently apropos to state emphatically that contempt for the phrase "art for art's sake" does not solve nor eliminate the problem of fitting or relating the æsthetic aspect of experience to one's total view of life. Because then a sensationalist art-for-art's-sake point of view results in oversimplification. Problems of æsthetics cannot be ruled off the agenda; to rule them off merely advertises one's own intellectual sloth.

CHAPTER III

Humanism

JUST as there have been extremes resulting from the divorcement of the æsthetic category, so have opposite extremes arisen from a divorcement of the functional category. The former extremism has created the demand for literature with no purpose outside of itself; the latter extremism has resulted in the demand for literature with a purpose—with so much purpose that everything else in it is bound to be sacrificed; in other words, it produces the demand for didactic literature.

Roman Catholicism gives birth to one form of functional extremism, demanding usually that literature be pressed into the service of Catholic theology and dogma. Thus, literature would illustrate "Catholic" truths, and organize faith in them. It would demand that the approach to character shall not contradict "Catholic" truths. It would therefore have to represent man as possessing an immortal soul, and the consequent analysis would have to be on the basis of "rational" psychology, which the Church would support. Furthermore, in cruder hands, literature would enforce Catholic moral codes, and even Catholic political and social policies; it would thus have to conform to the pernicious prejudices of the Legion of Decency, and fly the noisy banner of Catholic Action. From a Catholic viewpoint, the highest form of drama would be the moral one, in which the soul and the spirit triumph over the World, the Flesh, and the Devil. In brief, this would be literature with a moral purpose, and moral purpose would rest on a strictly developed theological, philosophical, and dogmatic basis. We should be arguing out of bounds, however, if we insisted that no literature has been produced by Catholics in contemporary times; we have, to disprove such a contention, the unique poetry of Francis Thompson. However, we can recognize the value of that poetry without subscribing to Catholicism or being in any way tainted by it, just as we can appreciate Milton's *Paradise Lost* without subscribing to Milton's theology and cosmology. In any case, Catholic literature of value is, in my judgment, rather the exception than the rule today.

Closely akin to the Catholic view of literature,

and sharing assumptions with it, are the literary Humanists, whose most representative spokesmen have been Paul Elmer More and the late Irving Babbitt. Literary Humanism, like Catholicism, posits a basically dualistic view of man and the universe, and assumes free will. Criticizing contemporary thought, life, and literature, it has stood in intransigeant opposition to almost the entire course of modern literature; and the basis of this opposition is that modern literature has usually lacked centrality because it has ignored the ethical core of human experience. Literary Humanism contends that modern literature has been, with notably few exceptions, romantic—that is to say, based on emotionalism, impulse, and expansionism, rather than on discipline, reason, and will; that it has failed to represent the essential dignity of man. In consequence, literature has wallowed in pits of materialism and humanitarianism. Literature, according to this school, must be based on sound models, must embody the best that mankind has thought and experienced. Sound models—whenever the literary Humanists have been able to find such a rarity—were patterns to be imitated; and a formula was thereby decreed for the creation of literary masterpieces.

Some years back, the literary Humanists issued

a "challenging" symposium, *Humanism and America,* edited by Norman Foerster (Farrar and Rinehart). One of the contributors, Harry Hayden Clark, wrote in his paper, "Pandora's Box in American Fiction," that "there is evidence, nevertheless, that the novel is no longer hostile to the specifically human destiny of normal humanity, no longer oblivious to that rare beauty which is the by-product of the struggle by which a noble character imposes order on the chaos of natural desire and approaches the imaginative ideal of a life richly varied, finely poised, and of exalted happiness." This statement, besides being rather grandiloquent, is a pæan in praise of an almost nonexistent literature celebrating "joyous centrality." The final appeal, in such a literature, is to moral authority and to a universalized moral order in the world which is apprehended by "intuition." But Dr. Babbitt's "intuition" is merely traditional conscience wrapped in one of his dried-up definitions, and connected with an antiquated free will.

The outlook of literary Humanism is narrowly academic. It demands a literature of negation and denial. Its assumptions are, on one hand, extra-literary; and, on the other, a string of definitions set in opposition to and denial of all the basic trends in modern thought. The Humanist assumption of dualism is built upon the creaking framework of an antiquated traditional philosophy. The doctrine of free will flies feebly in the face of modern social thought and psychology. Yet such are the fetters of dead absolutes in which they would enchain the creative imagination! If literature be unruly in such chains, it must not break them; accepting its chains, it must practise restraint. Like the Catholics, the literary Humanists desired that literature be the handmaiden of whatever they assumed as the Supreme Good; and to those of us for whom supernaturalism and idealism are dead and buried with all the philosophical and theological aliases of God, such an attitude is merely irrelevant.

Hence we challenge the primary postulates of literary Humanism, holding them to be untenable, incapable of demonstration. And even were they tenable and demonstrable, they would still be meaningless and irrelevant. For, if the basic "ground" of the universe be God, or Spirit, or a Moral Prerogative, and the nature of the world be dualistic, with spirit distinguished and separated from matter and placed in a different and higher realm, the result is a duplex apartment, each level of which operates in accordance with its own laws, and to its own purposes. The upstairs apartment works to its "spiritual" ends, and these ends are distinct from those downstairs and in the cellar. Between them there is an impasse, and all that the Catholics and the literary Humanists can do toward breaking through this impasse is to hurl empty words at it. And so, when they demand that literature growing out of the life, the pressures, and the needs downstairs and in the cellar be hitched to the ends and the purposes of the spirits upstairs, they are talking about spooks.[2]

[2] The social and political position based on the viewpoint of literary Humanism is more objectionable than its literary position. I do not deal with it here because I am confining myself to literature. Lest some take my omission of this aspect of Humanism to be an affirmation of it, I may say here that the political position of Humanism—best stated in Dr. Babbitt's *Democracy and Leadership*—defends the status quo, argues against democratic principles, condemns strikes, views the issues in the modern world as a clear-cut fight between Christianity and Communism, and is unqualifiedly repugnant and reactionary.

CHAPTER IV

Left-Wing Dualism

ON THE opposite side of the political fence we
find various revolutionary critics whose functional
extremism has been almost as grievous as that of
the literary Humanists. Tendencies classifiable under this extremism are usually described as "leftist."
Leftism reveals two noticeable streams in revolutionary criticism which, starting from opposite
poles, usually meet in the same rut.

One of these may be called the school of revolutionary sentimentalism. Anti-rational to the core,
it usually fights criticism with epithets, and struggles against ideas as "petty bourgeois abstractions."
It demands a literature of simplicity to the point
of obviousness, and even of downright banality.
Crying for songs of "stench and sweat," it tends to
idealize the "worker" and "the worker-writer,"
producing overdrawn pictures of both. It belligerently sinks all critical criteria under the appeal of

29

generalized terms like "the masses"; and it seems to assume that revolutionary and proletarian literature will develop in pristine glory, beauty, and simplicity without benefit of antecedent influences. It fails to recognize and distinguish the myriad influences that enter into the living current of contemporary literature, permitting these to affect judgments *unconsciously* and hence uncritically. Perhaps the most famous representative of this tendency in America is Michael Gold.[3]

[3] The school of revolutionary sentimentalism was represented by Mr. Gold during the American Writers' Congress in April, 1935. See *The American Writers' Congress*, Discussions and Proceedings, edited by Henry Hart, pp. 166–7, International Publishers. I quote Mr. Gold: "I think that the tone of many of our papers this morning showed that our literary movement is in danger of becoming a petty bourgeois movement. I think we must guard against that. It cannot become that. It must not become that. It is our main task to see that a strong working class is developed in the United States to lead the revolutionary vanguard. We may not lead it. So I think one of the basic tasks of every writer is to stimulate and encourage and help the growth of proletarian literature which is written by workers. We must realize that only this literature can answer these intellectual abstractions into which petty bourgeois people fall. A great body of proletarian literature will show the concrete facts. . . . We must use this as the final answer we can give to the intellectual abstractions of the bourgeoisie."

These remarks suggest several comments. (1) Without intellectual abstractions, it is impossible to think. (2) Facts, unless they are correlated and interpreted in generalizations (which is to say, in abstractions), are meaningless. (3) If worker writers are gathered around a professional writer, and he reads their work, criticizes it, and offers suggestions, how are these criticisms and suggestions to be offered without the use of abstractions? (4) One way that workers are helped to be writers is by a body of critical writing which establishes a literary atmosphere in which not only their work but also that of others is received. How can this be done without the use of abstractions? (5) It is therefore apparent

LEFT-WING DUALISM

The second tendency is that of a mechanically deterministic "Marxism." It usually assumes implicitly, if not explicitly, that literature follows economics obediently and directly. It approaches literature from the outside with a narrow set of absolutes and abstractions. In America it is perhaps most notably represented by Granville Hicks.

It will be more profitable for us to examine these two tendencies in revolutionary criticism in some detail than it would be to analyze at length the

---

that no kind of literature, including "proletarian," can be understood, assimilated, or appreciated, without the use of intellectual abstractions.

These are axiomatic matters which are known to any person who thinks. However, I may quote a reference here on the use of abstractions: "The economic categories are only the theoretical expressions, the abstractions, of the social relations of production." (Karl Marx, *The Poverty of Philosophy*, tr. by H. Quelch, p. 119. Charles Kerr, Chicago.) It turns out, therefore, that Mr. Gold, in inveighing against abstractions, is using abstractions in his inveighing, doing this in order to enforce the view of a man who himself used abstractions. Marx's abstractions were not all invented by him; some of them were developed from Ricardo, for instance. Therefore . . . !

The attitude which Michael Gold sponsors, culturally, in America is similar to the one which, in politics, Lenin slashingly fought in Russia over thirty years ago—a struggle epitomized in the phrase "consciousness versus spontaneity." Lenin gave "certificates of mental poverty" to the adherents of "spontaneity," on whom his revolutionary classic, *What Is To Be Done*, is a relentless attack. However, I most confess that, in this volume, one of the abstractions which Lenin used was the word *consciousness*, and there is some point to the argument that the word is a petty bourgeois abstraction; I do not believe that I could deny such a contention, because I know of no proof that Lenin invented the word. All of which reminds me of a remark by Karl Marx: "The educator must himself be educated." (*Theses on Feuerbach*, printed as an appendix in *Ludwig Feuerbach* by Frederick Engels, p. 74, International Publishers.)

functional extremism of literary Humanism. Revolutionary extremism is traveling in the same direction as we are, and it becomes an impediment that we meet the more frequently because it is more often placed in our road. And since it is an extremism hitched to a progressive force—whereas literary Humanism is tied to a regressive one—it requires correction. Such an extremism as literary Humanism is wrong on premises more fundamental even than those of literary "leftism"; and the nature of these premises has been revealed.

Revolutionary extremists have preached their one-sided functionalism under the banner of "Marxism" and "Marxist-Leninism." Here I may state some of the bases for this extremism, and—as my argument and analysis develop—concern myself with more specific points and concrete details. In his *Theses on Feuerbach* Marx wrote [4] that "the philosophers have only *interpreted* the world in various ways; the point, however, is to change it." [5] Transferred into literature, this remark has been utilized for such an argument as the following: Bourgeois literature has only reflected the world. Proletarian literature must be an advance

[4] In *Ludwig Feuerbach*, by F. Engels, p. 75 (International Publishers).
[5] In all quoted statements, whenever the italics are mine, I shall indicate this parenthetically.

32

on bourgeois literature by changing the world. It must be consonant with the Marxian dictum that word and deed, theory and action correspond. Proletarian literature must therefore be a literature of action. This view has been expressed by Philip Rahv, one of the present editors of *The Partisan Review and Anvil*, as consistently as by anyone in America. Several years ago he made his bow [6] in the field of revolutionary criticism with this thesis: Bourgeois literature was rapidly sinking into its grave. It would be supplanted by proletarian literature. Proletarian literature had not, however, more than begun. Until it developed, the effect of literature was to produce an Aristotelian katharsis, a "purging by pity and fear." This was a leisure-class product, both as a theory and as an effect. The Greek aristocrat could go to see a tragedy, be purged by pity and fear, recognize the laws of necessity that operated from the will and passions of Greek gods and goddesses, and then return home to contemplate; while his slaves and artisans did the practical work of society.

To this katharsis, which Rahv recognized as a legitimate effect from literature, proletarian litera-

[6] "The Literary Class War," *New Masses*, August, 1932. This was a first piece and Mr. Rahv in his subsequent critical pieces has not followed the "line" laid down by such a thesis. To the contrary, he has increasingly been developing an anti-"leftist" point of view.

ture would add a new element, carrying literature to a higher plane, and permitting the correspondence of word and deed; that new element would be *militancy*. The conscious utilization of literature as an instrument of revolutionary action flows from the Marxian concept of the class struggle. Thus, Edwin Seaver has argued [7] that the terms bourgeois literature and proletarian literature "represent the same struggle being conducted on the cultural front, and at the same time as the struggle on the economic front." Literature as action is represented in such slogans as "Literature is a weapon in the class struggle." And frequently in pushing forward and defending these conceptions, critics and "theoreticians" have seemed to imply that such slogans exhaust the rôle and the functions of literature; and, in addition, that they square perfectly with the implications to be found in the general body of Marxist knowledge and principles.

Revolutionary critics are here speaking of that aspect of literature which I have deemed the functional. It can be formally stated that the problem of the relation of the functional aspect of literature to the æsthetic can be resolved by fitting the latter into a framework of Marxian principles.

[7] "The Proletarian Novel," in *The American Writers' Congress*, p. 102.

Granville Hicks [8] has recognized this problem, suggesting that in the past it has gone unresolved by such critics as Upton Sinclair, and Floyd Dell and others of the *Old Masses* group. Now, however, with a basis of Marxist criticism established, "we are ready to achieve a far more adequate unification." John Strachey, in *Literature and Dialectical Materialism,* failed to find an adequate correlation between the functional and the æsthetic, and so managed to develop what is more or less a double standard for literature: he perceived the writer as Marxist and revolutionary, and the writer as writer, seeking to create adequate images for his own vision. According to Mr. Hicks, [9] however, Strachey has modified that conception, though I do not know exactly how. In any case, it is almost a truism to remark that a formal statement describing how this resolution of the problem is managed, and a subsequent demonstration of the resolution in terms of concrete critical applications, are two distinct efforts, and the second of these demands thoroughgoing application and investigation.

V. F. Calverton, in *The Liberation of American*

[8] "The Dialectics of the Development of Marxist Criticism," in *The American Writers' Congress,* p. 98.
[9] *Op. cit.,* p. 96.

Literature (Scribner's), deals with this problem. He writes:

"The revolutionary proletarian critic does not aim to underestimate literary craftsmanship. What he contends is simply that literary craftsmanship is not enough. The craftsmanship must be utilized to create objects of revolutionary meaning. . . . Revolutionary meanings without literary craftsmanship constitute as hopeless a combination from the point of view of the radical critic as literary craftsmanship without revolutionary purpose. If proletarian literature fails in so many instances in America, it is not because it is propagandistic . . . but because it is lacking in qualities of craftsmanship. . . . Granted the craftsmanship, our aim should be to make art serve man as a thing of action and not man serve art as a thing of escape."

All that Calverton is saying here is that a writer must know how to write. And with the crudest reasoning he facilely establishes categories as an escape from actually coming to serious grips with this problem. He reduces æsthetics to simple craftsmanship, and conceives it as one category; and content is then polarized with it in an elementary fashion. In addition, literature is dichotomized into a literature of service and of escape.

In *The New Masses*, Isidor Schneider [10] has asked

10 "By Way of Review," by Isidor Schneider, *New Masses*, Jan. 14, 1936.

the question, "What is Marxist criticism?" At-tempting a "partial answer," he selected several books as specific examples, one of them being *The Tale of Genji* by Lady Murasaki. He confessed that if he had been reviewing such a volume ten years ago—in his pre-Marxist days—he would have of-fered certain statements concerning the literary value of this work, and that these would have re-ferred to the establishment of moods, characteriza-tion, and the like. Now, as a Marxist, he is able to make the same comments on the literary value of this novel that he would have made ten years ago; but he now has additional remarks to offer. These tell us that *The Tale of Genji* reflects the decline of an era, that it is a picture of decadence; which—according to Mr. Schneider—explains its melan-choly tone. He says also that he would proceed to show that behind the characters, events, and situ-ations represented in the narrative there is a class struggle. One of his conclusions reads: "Such a commentary [as the one paraphrased] may slightly alter judgments upon a book. To establish that a book is the product of a ruling class and represents it alone, that it leaves the greater part of the life of its time untouched, does delimit its boundaries. We know then that we can view the book as a picture of Japanese life only in a restricted sense.

But in essentials the esthetic judgment is unaltered. Through such a treatment nothing is subtracted and something is added. Accurate points of social reference are fixed: and its impact, at least for many readers, is deepened."

While these remarks are slightly platitudinous, I quote them because they are most revealing and illustrative. First of all, Mr. Schneider practically admits that there is no real relationship between æsthetics and a Marxist interpretation. For his Marxism does not, in any of its essentials, alter the æsthetic judgments that he would have made on the work before he became a Marxist. Thus, unless he contends that ten years ago he was an "unconscious" Marxist, he implicitly denies that an important relationship here exists. Marxism is—if Mr. Schneider's remarks be correct—a set of interpretations to be added on top of æsthetic judgments in order that accurate points of social reference "be fixed," thereby deepening meanings.

If this view is a sound Marxist one, it leaves no avenue open for a consideration of the natural history of æsthetic standards; and Marxism, as a method of genetic analysis seeking to uncover points of the social and economic origin of æsthetic standards, cannot function consistently. For, if Mr. Schneider means what he says, there is no im-

portant and essential connection between the two;
his idea is implicitly that Marxism is a superimposi-
tion upon the æsthetic or literary aspects of a work
of literature. Further, it might be noted that the
social implications which Mr. Schneider draws out
of this book are of a most general nature. They are
true not only for *The Tale of Genji* but also for a
wide variety of other books and other cultural
phenomena in an entire period and over a wide
geographical area. An ordinarily intelligent reader,
even if he were non-Marxist in terms of
Schneider's conception of Marxism, should be able
to perceive as much from a normally careful reading of Lady Murasaki's story. Hence we might say
that, as Marxism, such an interpretation is about as
useful as would be to science the work of a man
who was forever re-proving, by experiment, that
the formula for water is H_2O.[11]

These remarks should explain to us the failure of
some of our "Marxist" critics to qualify sufficiently for their tasks. They separate æsthetic and

[11] "Michel Angelo said of himself: 'My teaching will procreate a great
number of ignoramuses.' Unfortunately this prophecy was fulfilled. Nowadays it is Marx's teaching which is procreating ignoramuses. Of course
that is the fault not of Marx but of those who utter so many follies in
his name. If such follies are to be avoided, we must gain a true understanding of the methodological value of historical materialism." George
Plekhanov, *Fundamental Problems of Marxism*, pp. 24–25. International
Publishers.

social implications, superimposing one upon the other, and discovering, for the latter, general and familiar information of a sociological and economic nature.

Here we have discovered the problem which besets—or will beset—all those whose main concern is literary and æsthetic theory and the problems of criticism in their generalized features. Suffice it, at this point, to state the problem.

CHAPTER V

The Literature of the Past in the Present

THERE are certain obstacles in literary criticism
which have often been slid over or ignored in revolutionary criticism. Some of these obstacles can
best be indicated by a reference to what is now
known as the literature of the past. Often, the
slogan that literature is propaganda has been defended by the statement that great literary artists
of the past were propagandists.

Mr. Granville Hicks, in *The Great Tradition*,
implicitly develops this contention. In order to prove
the revolutionary ancestry and heritage of contemporary American revolutionary writers, he suggests by a long and rather mechanical analysis that
the great tradition in American writing has been
built up by writers who were concerned with the
problems of their day and age; only, his definition
of the problems, used as a measuring rod, is to gen-
eralize basic economic and social conditions. From

41

this he derives the curious conclusion that the great tradition is made up mainly of failures and partial failures who did not manage to come to grips sufficiently with the problems of their day and age, as he, *a posteriori,* views those problems in generalities.

A recent little book on Shakespeare [12] presents an analogous argument. The author culls the Shakespearian plays for passages proving that Shakespeare sided with the bourgeoisie and against the aristocracy, and—as a corollary—favored Protestantism as against the Catholicism of the nobles. From these culling exercises Mr. Morrow reaches the following conclusion: "When all else is said of Shakespeare, the fact remains that in expressing this class he belonged with the movement forward. His work, as the entire renaissance, was on the side of life."

A book attempting to prove such a thesis calls for certain comments. It is almost a foregone conclusion that a great artist will be "on the side of life." Second, whether he was, formally, on the side of life or death does not now, centuries later, give us the firmest ground for argument, because we know

[12] *Where Shakespeare Stood: His Part in the Crucial Struggles of His Day,* by Donald Morrow. With an Introduction by Granville Hicks. Casanova Press, Milwaukee.

that great artists, like Dostoevski and Balzac, in their formal sympathies and formal ideology, were on the side of "death." Further, the life issues in Shakespeare's plays do not retain the immediacy and the importance that they may have possessed for his original audiences in his own lifetime. Finally, the implication to be drawn from Mr. Morrow's conclusion—that the artist today should be on the side of life—can, it seems to me, be driven home more forcibly, effectively, and economically, by a discussion of immediate issues and problems. I doubt the revolutionary efficacy of Mr. Morrow's indirect appeal to prove that the artist of 1936 should be on the side of life.

I once heard an important young contemporary revolutionary writer, in a speech defending propaganda in literature, illustrate his general thesis by saying that Shakespeare was a propagandist who defended British imperialism. Does this statement mean that *Macbeth* and *Hamlet* are today a part of the ideological defense of the British Empire? Should we say that the value of *Macbeth* is that, along with the Singapore naval base, it is a bulwark of the far-flung Empire? Or should we say that one of the reasons why *Macbeth* possesses human worth for us today is that it is a profound and tragic dramatization of the phenomenon of human ambition for power and glory? Similarly, should we say that *Hamlet* carries coals to Newcastle? Or —instead of this—that one of its values is that it is a moving and dramatic representation of a man's disillusionment and indecision?

Human experience is, in some aspects, recurrent; this is true, at least, of Occidental man. In other words, there are some strains of similarity, some recognizable repetitions, in the patterns of experience between what men in the Western world felt and experienced many years ago, and what men today sometimes feel and experience. In discovering the world, each man discovers many of the things that some of his forbears have discovered. Today, many men who have been glutted with the aim of achieving power often feel somewhat as Macbeth felt when fortune went against him. Similarly, men today have sometimes given public or private utterance to sentiments like those of Hamlet. And one value of these two plays is that they succeed in representing, dramatically, certain recurrent factors in the experience of Western man. And if this analysis be correct, it demands some extension of ideas and references on the part of those who have so crassly interpreted the slogan that all literature is propaganda.

Dickens has sometimes been presented as another case in point to prove a simple interpretation of this formula. The platitude with which Mr. Morrow flirts can easily be demonstrated as true in this case. Dickens did not—in a simple language —ignore his own times. In considering him today, however, we often note that what interests us most in him is not Dickens the propagandist; and the discovery that he was a propagandist, therefore, does not exhaust his value as a novelist who retains his worth in our own times. Today, much of Dickens as a propagandist is "dated." His successors have furnished infinitely more useful propaganda than we may find in his books. There are other values in Dickens, and when we read him today, we generally do so because of these other values. He re-creates a sense of the life of his time, and in doing so he gives us characters who exist in their own right as literary representations of the human species. An additional value is his pictorial quality, his descriptive ability, his extraordinary talent for describing scenes and objects in a manner sufficiently vivid to provide us, imaginatively, with a sense of their contours and their "feel." When we discover such qualities in Dickens, we describe him as containing virtues that are indubitably æsthetic, and we say that one of the reasons why Dickens survives is that in his works he has presented the formal objects that provide æsthetic gratification.

If this be true, a conclusion is suggested. Certain works of literature possess a human worth and a carry-over power which endow them with a relatively inherent persistence-value after they have been divorced from the material conditions and the society out of which they have been created. And this conclusion leads us to the corollary that there is a relative objective validity to some works of formal art. And, further, we are led to conclude that some works that we now view as the literature of the present will, with the passage of time, also be added to the literature of the past. When that occurs, we shall necessarily be faced with the problem of considering their persistence-value. This being the case, it is—to say the least—uneconomical to disregard or slur over these features of contemporary literary works; when we do so we are merely strewing errors in the stream of literary influences and judgments—errors that someone in the future will have to correct. And, more important, we are missing certain essential features of a work of literature.

CHAPTER VI

Marx on the Relative Æsthetic Validity of Literature

How do these conclusions square with Marx and Marxism? There is printed evidence to suggest that Marx recognized this aspect of literature. In his note on Greek mythology in *A Contribution to the Critique of Political Economy,* he wrote: "It is well known that certain periods of highest development of art stand in no direct connection with the general development of society, nor with the material basis and the skeleton structure of its organization." Following this statement, he cites Greek art as an example. He suggests that the ideological content of Greek art was the direct product of the Greek way of life, and that an art founded on mythological conceptions, like those of the Greek ideology, is obviously unrepeatable in an industrial age. It might be noted that there is within his suggestion the basis for one of the state-

ments which "leftists" have often reduced to a
wearing platitude, and then misapplied. A writer
cannot misuse the conceptions of the past as the
criterion for his interpretations of the present.[13]

In other words, if he is to live and become a vital
and progressive influence as a literary artist, he

---

[13] It is interesting to note that this truism is sometimes neglected in
concrete instances. Maxwell Anderson's drama *Winterset* is a case in
point. Mr. Anderson attempted to present both a play based on the tragic
conception of necessity and a contemporary social drama whose source is
clearly the Sacco-Vanzetti case. As Marx suggested, there was a reason,
ideologically, for Greek art, and it found its source in Greek mythology.
The element of necessity in Greek tragedy was drawn from this source.
Mr. Anderson reveals how this may become distorted and reasonless when
it is separated from its source and ingressed in a modern play. The necessity which plays Fate and demands a tragic ending in *Winterset* does
not focus through the specific motivation of the characters. It is laid
over the specific motivations, as additional ones. The result is that on
one side the characters are motivated by specific social stimuli; on the
other hand, their motivation stems from generalized categories—hate,
destiny, love, revenge. These two sources of motivation become en-
tangled, and as a result there is an internal contradiction in the play
which destroys the possibility (at least in my case) of "believing" in
Mr. Anderson's play as a reproduction and representation of life. The
tragedy happens, in the final act, not from the necessities that grow
out of the particular set of relationships in which the characters find
themselves; rather the tragedy results from the necessities demanded by
Mr. Anderson's determination to motivate modern characters in a modern
setting with a classical conception of tragedy that is extracted from its
consummate ideological background. As a consequence, there is no noticeable internal reason why the hero should walk out to a death from the
barking guns of gangsters; he goes to his death because the author's
preconception of tragic necessity forces him to. Thus I submit *Winterset*
as a clear-cut case of what Marx meant when he said that art founded
on the ideology of an age cannot be motivated, in a succeeding age, from
that past and dead ideology. When, however, that ideology, or part of
it, is still alive in the sense that it remains an active social influence in
the present, the situation is different. But this is not the case in *Winterset*.

cannot escape into the past. However much Mr. Thornton Wilder may require lectures on this truism, most contemporary writers of worth do not need it.

But to continue, Marx then writes: "The difficulty is not in grasping the idea that Greek art and epos are bound up with certain forms of social development. It rather lies in understanding why they still constitute with us a source of æsthetic enjoyment and in certain respects prevail as one standard and model beyond attainment." The mere fact that he spoke in this way of Greek art as a source of æsthetic enjoyment suggests that he recognized a certain objective validity in a work of art. He goes on to say that the Greeks were "normal children" representing the social childhood of the human race at its best; and that just as we as individuals look back on childhood, so do we as a race look back with enjoyment on the social childhood of the human race. It is apparent that our enjoyment of the products of the social childhood of the human race has no direct and immediate use-value to us in the press of our times, is of no direct help in solving the crying problems and issues of our day.

A few years ago, Granville Hicks contributed a series of articles to the *New Masses* under the title of "Revolution and the Novel," discussing, among other things, the historical novel. He suggested [14] two "essential qualities" by which the historical novel should be judged: authenticity and relevance; and he defined the latter as "relevance to the fundamental interests of the author and his readers" and "relevance to the contemporary situation, interests, and demands of the working class." Since the historical novel brings a sense of the life of a past era into the present, we can extend his criterion of relevance to an æsthetic appreciation of æsthetic objects from the past. For after all, whether we view the past through historical novels written contemporaneously, or through documents, works of art, and the like that have survived from the past, it remains true that we are viewing the past. And our view of the past is from the vantage point of the present. Also we view the past, in terms of my categories here, for functional or for æsthetic purposes, or for both. Marx's note on Greek mythology here refers to art in the past, viewed æsthetically, as well as for what it might illustrate in the working of social processes. However, his judgment of Greek art does not meet Granville Hicks' test of relevance, if we extend that from the judg-

14 "The Past and the Future"—first article in the series, *New Masses*, April 3, 1934.

ment of the historical novel to the judgment of the art of the past. For it is not very conceivable that an appreciation of Greek art, as illustrating the social childhood of the human race, and because of its enjoyment, can have the kind of "relevance to the contemporary situation, interests, and demands of the working class" that Mr. Hicks would require. Here, when his statement is logically extended as I have extended it, Mr. Hicks seems not to agree with Marx. I agree with Marx rather than with Mr. Hicks.

Thus I conclude that, accepting my analysis, we derive a kind of experience from this consideration and contemplation of Greek art and culture which is, at least in part, æsthetic. In other words, we can say that Greek art, in providing formal objects of æsthetic experience, retains some objective validity today; and we have here implications drawn from Marx himself, which lend support to our generalization.

There is a noticeable tendency, in works of literature and in works of thought as well, to undergo a shifting of status after they have been sufficiently removed, in time, from their original setting. They tend to become reduced in their functional status —sometimes to lose it entirely; and they continue to interest us for reasons that are preponderantly, if not wholly, æsthetic. The problems which such works treat have been either solved or washed aside in the passage of history. Their orientation has sunken into the past, lost in the process of changing societies. Functional references are thus eliminated, superseded, revised downwards, proven inadequate.

Plato is an example. His thought is the product of a view of the world peculiar to a particular class in a definite social system. It is the product of a slave-owning society where intellectual production was socially separated from material production, to become the prerogative of a special leisure class. To the Greek autocracy the highest type of thought was pure contemplation.

Thus, to take an example from *The Republic:* "We were enquiring into the nature of absolute justice and into the character of the perfectly just, and into injustice and the perfectly unjust, that we might have an ideal. We were to look at these in order that we might judge of our own happiness and unhappiness according to the standard which they exhibited and the degree in which we resembled them, but not with any view of showing that they could exist in fact."

This example is most illustrative of our point. The ideal, or norm, here refers not to experience in process, but to a fixed ideal standard.

Hence conduct is to be judged by reference to static ideals which are beyond the process of change. The method of conceiving and attaining an apprehension of these standards is not a knowledge process; rather it is cognition, refined by logical methods. The knowledge process, as we know it, is cut up, and pure knowledge is attained by a dependence upon only one aspect of that process. Ideals are shown not to exist in fact; they occupy a different compartment in the Platonic world. Today, in an age imbued with the spirit and method of modern science, and approached within a materialistic framework, such a viewpoint becomes fantastic. We cannot demonstrate ideal entities scientifically. We cannot test conduct and the solution of problems in the world of action by reference to these ideal entities, because they are of a different world. Whereas we today use reference to experience as a corrective of pure definitions, Plato would use definitions as a corrective of experience. There is here a separation of the functional and the æsthetic. We must, in consequence, reject Plato's method; we must, indeed, reject many elements of his thought because they do not retain their functional utility in our world. Plato was a great primary thinker who set the tone of philosophical thought for centuries. By now he has lost ground, and continues to lose it, because the basis of his thought has been washed from under him. Thus we are more and more inclined to view him as an object of historical curiosity, as a poet and dramatist who used ideas for characters and protagonists. In consequence, we say that today the value we find in Plato is more predominantly æsthetic than it is functional, and the dialogues continue to shift in status from the presentation of ideas that are usable, in the broad sense of that word, to dramas of ideas that possess enduring æsthetic charm. Plato, then, becomes a clear-cut case of the tendency of thought to lose its functional application and to shift over into the category of æsthetics.

I present this analysis both as an essential illustration of the constituents of the æsthetic element in literature, and as a proof that the recognition of the relative objective validity of literature as a branch of the fine arts is not inconsistent with Marxism as a body of thought and a method of analysis.

CHAPTER VII

Tradition in Thought

THERE are certain statements which are consistent with a Marxian hypothesis, and which can be applied to matters of artistic and literary creation. One is that the objects and ends of our activities and the problems of life and society exert a controlling and directive influence over the thoughts and the actions of men. This means that the objective conditions, so-called, tend to condition what can be done. They constitute the channel through which our thought, often unconsciously, tends to flow. The development and the emphasis in formal thought in particular directions naturally follow. Nature and society—which is a part of Nature, and through which civilized man must see and apprehend Nature—present the objects, the conditioning factors, and the ends of thought. The development of art and literature, then, is not an independent process existing in a vacuum. This is a truism. There is a difference, however, between recognizing that objective conditions determine thought, and knowing the precise process or manner in which this determination proceeds. The development between end products in a society (like art, thought, and literature) from the basic material and economic relationships is not even and regular. To Marx and Engels, those who treated it as even and regular were "vulgarizing pedlars" of materialism. Engels wrote pertinently in *Ludwig Feuerbach:*

"Every ideology, however, once it has arisen, develops in connection with the given concept material, and develops this material further; otherwise it would cease to be ideology, that is, occupation with thoughts as with independent entities, developing independently and subject only to their own laws. That the material life conditions of the persons inside whose heads this thought process goes on, in the last resort determine the course of this process, remains of necessity unknown to these persons, for otherwise there would be an end to all ideology."

In other words, the relationship between economics and ideology cannot be graphed as a straight line between two points, nor expressed in a simple equation showing direct relationships, one leading head-on into the other. To write and to think as if such an achievement were possible, as if it could be made into a relatively abstract description of the working out of relationships in societies, is to be guilty of crass determinism. And to utilize such a crass simplification in the name of Marx and Engels is to pervert their ideas in a way that seems foreign to their very spirit.

When Marx and Engels traced and described the influence of economics on social processes, they did not do so in order to exclude other factors that influence social processes—factors like ideals, art, culture. To quote Engels in *Ludwig Feuerbach* again:

"The great basic thought that the world is not to be comprehended as a complex of ready-made *things*, but as a complex of *processes*, in which the things apparently stable no less than their mind-images in our heads, the concepts, go through an uninterrupted change of coming into being and passing away, in which, in spite of all seeming accidents and of all temporary retrogression, a progressive development asserts itself in the end."

And

"Men make their own history, whatever its outcome may be, in that each person follows his own consciously desired end, and it is precisely the resultant of these many wills operating in different directions and of their manifold effects upon the outer world that constitutes history. Thus it is also a question of what the many individuals desire. The will is determined by passion or deliberation. But the levers which immediately determine passion or deliberation are of very different kinds. Partly they may be external objects, partly ideal motives, ambition, 'enthusiasms for truth and justice', personal hatred or even purely individual whims of all kinds."

Engels continues by suggesting that these motivating factors never quite produce the results intended, and that in relation to the total result they are of secondary significance. However, to be of secondary significance does not mean that they are of no significance; anyone familiar with scientific method will realize that though a factor in a causal nexus may be of secondary significance, it is still of significance and cannot be ignored.

In considering Marx and Engels, and seeking to apply their ideas to literature, then, we may not legitimately use them to prove views opposite to those they intended.[15] In addition, we must view their writings in relation to their purpose and their times. They both wrote in a period when the tradi-

[15] "According to the materialist conception of history the determining element in history is *ultimately* the production and reproduction in real life. More than this neither Marx nor I have ever asserted. If therefore somebody twists this into the statement that the economic element is the *only* determining one, he transforms it into a meaningless, abstract and absurd phrase." *Marx-Engels, Selected Correspondence*, No. 213, p. 475 —Engels to J. Bloch, London, 21 September, 1890. International Publishers.

tion of philosophical idealism was the most powerful intellectual current in Germany. German philosophers were concerned with such questions as what is the "ground" of the universe, and their answer was Spirit. And spirit meant an extra-experiential entity and force; that is, it was a new word for an old God. An implication of this doctrine is that spirit is the motivating force in both the universe and society. Marx's materialism was a revolt from this doctrine. For Marx, material forces were the mainspring of the historical process; in society these material forces were predominantly economic in character. And since he wrote in opposition to German idealism in its manifold forms, he had to make a particularly strong emphasis on economic relationships. From what we have already said of the manner in which thought is conditioned, it is apparent that the German philosophical tradition would itself have been a conditioning factor in this emphasis. Marx did not mean that economics was the sole factor; and Lenin, in *What Is To Be Done* (International) criticized those who forged slogans growing out of such simplifications. Thus Lenin criticized the simplified slogan: "Politics always obediently follows economics."

Granville Hicks, in *The Great Tradition*, says in reference to the writers of Dreiser's generation:

"As we shall see, there is not a single writer of the middle generation whose work is not vitiated by faults that may be more or less directly traced to the instability of the basic economic situation." In one sense, there is probably no writer who ever lived about whom such a remark cannot be made. All writers are the children of their age, of their times, and of the past out of which their age and their times have emerged; thus it is obvious that a writer will possess not only certain of the strengths of his age, but also some of its weaknesses. In this respect, Mr. Hicks' remark is a platitude.

It is to be challenged, further, because it introduces a method of criticism that flies the banner of Marxism, but in actual procedure utilizes a method that is mechanical. For when Mr. Hicks applies his theory in detail, he uses it as a measuring standard for the novelists of Dreiser's generation, and consequently tends to allow this standard to intrude between the books he considers and the judgments which he as a critic should make of them. The implicit meaning of Hicks' statement is this: Literature obediently follows economics. The basic weaknesses of the economic situation in any period produce weaknesses in the literature of that period. That literature is therefore a failure, or a partial failure. This statement contains within itself, implicitly, the weakness of a whole side of contemporary left-wing and revolutionary criticism and book-reviewing. It posits indirect relationships as direct; simplifies the general structure of conceptions of the working of social processes and the interconnections that go to make up the inside of this process; and ends by using an economic yardstick for the placing and measuring of literature, thereby negating a fundamental function of criticism—that of judgment.[16]

Marx, then, conceived societies in motion, and he perceived that the factor of change is ever present in social relationships. Because of this factor, the effects of one set of relationships become causal factors for the next set, and thus there is ever evolving a whole network of influences; so that cultural manifestations, such as formal art, thought, and literature, which *may be* directly related to the basic material and economic relationships upon which a society is founded in one era, evolve away from that set of relationships as the

---

[16] An intellectual presentation always means not only what it says, but also what it leads to, what it involves in application and in extension with other ideas, and in reference to experience. And when we consider Mr. Hicks' statements in this light, we discover that, even though he has been described as the "foremost" Marxian literary critic in America, he nevertheless has the habit of disagreeing regularly with Marx and Lenin.

process unfolds with the passage of time, and they in turn become part of the network of causal factors and conditioning influences in the general stream of social tendencies and forces.

This description of the manner in which the status of cultural manifestations changes describes the general process in which thought, art, and literature possess a carry-over value—the precise value which must be extracted from tradition.[17] Tradition exists. It is a mighty social force, but it is inert. It may be turned into either a progressive or a regressive force. It has been impressed into the ideology, with modifications, from one epoch to the next, and it is not one lump of equal impact. When tradition is merely the weight of dead ideas and institutions which persist through inertia long past their period of usefulness, it needs to be exposed as such and destroyed. Where, on the contrary, tradition can still contribute elements to the enrichment of contemporary life, these must be extracted and assimilated. In any case, it should be

[17] Besides tradition, there is outside historical influence—that is, an influence coming to bear on the present ideology from a past historical epoch, or from a remote society, where there is no direct traditional line of influencings and interconnections between that past epoch or remote society and the ideology upon which this outside historical influence is brought to bear. In these terms, the influence of African primitive art on certain types of modern painting and sculpture might be described as within the category of "outside historic influence."

repeated that tradition does not form one lump of equal relevance or irrelevance.

Thus, for instance, the philosophy of Saint Thomas Aquinas is today a social influence, presented to us, directly and indirectly, in many ways. Particularly since Catholic Action has become noisy and militant, extending its range of effort over an international area, we must perceive the influence of Aquinas in its devious workings. The Catholic Church, and its leader, the Pope, present his ideas as part of the body of doctrine, dogma, thought, and methods which must be taken cognizance of as factors to be negated in solving a wide variety of contemporary problems. In addition, there is the phenomenon of neo-Thomism, and there are the contemporary philosophers and teachers of "philosophy" who present to students and women's clubs the idea that Saint Thomas thought out everything anyway, and so there is not much use for us to do any thinking.

The influence of Aquinas is a fact of some importance to us in our effort to understand the origins and formulations of contemporary problems, since it illustrates the uneven and irregular rather than the even and regular development of ideology. In considering the use of his ideas in the task of solving today's problems, it is not enough for us to say that his "weakness" was due to the weakness of the economic situation and forces of his times. Likewise, it is saying next to nothing to remark that he might have been all right for his time, but that for our time he is inadequate, irrelevant, and antiquated. Finally, we cannot dismiss him by saying that he is the official philosopher and theologian of the Roman Catholic Church, and that the Roman Catholic Church is an ally of the capitalist class and a defender of the status quo; and that therefore Aquinas is a hangover used to defend capitalism, and his thought non-proletarian. In short, it is inept to dismiss him with truisms and generalizations that have such a broad application that they refer not only to him but also to an infinity of other phenomena, ideological and material.

Rather we must—in dealing with Thomas Aquinas—consider not the origins of his thought merely, but their meaning today, their reference and relationship to the actual contemporary problems to which they are or may be applied. We must make judgments here, and the first judgment we make is in connection with his method, and with the fact that his method is advocated and utilized today, and that, in Catholic institutions of learning, successive generations are trained to apply it.

The Thomistic method is that of scholastic thought—the inductive method. It is based on the premise that there are first principles—universals or absolutes; and that the first appeal is to these absolutes. Positing an absolute, we shall find special instances illustrating it, and then we arrive at a conclusion. The conclusion is then referred to the external and objective world. The central "universal or absolute" is the Unprecedented First Cause of the universe—an omniscient and omnipotent God. For this the proof is twofold: from revelation and from logic.

Now the proof from revelation we can dismiss by appealing to science to show that the likelihood of God's revealing Himself is negligible, because the possibility that there is any God at all to reveal Himself is far removed from demonstrability. In considering the proof from logic, we shall find a contemporary disciple of Saint Thomas—an adept in his methods and his reasoning—finally falling back on the argument about the watch found on the desert island: there cannot be an effect without a cause, and therefore there must be a First Cause. In this argument, however, the word *cause* is used in a double sense, which de-

stroys the argument. It is argued that there cannot be accident in the universe, and that therefore, as there is a relationship in the present, there
must have been antecedent relationships that were
part of a causal nexus producing this present relationship. We say that there must have been some-
where an unprecedented First Cause to have orig-
inated the first relationship. We then argue that
this First Cause is the possessor of qualities that
have no connection with the way in which the
law of cause and effect works in the stream
of events in Nature. We attribute to this First
Cause omniscience and omnipotence; we describe
it as free from the necessities of causal relationships; and we conceive it as a spirit beyond the
realm of cause and effect as this law works out in
Nature. Thus we are proving the existence of God
by using the same word in two different senses.

But this is the method of Aquinas. He builds
a system wherein there is such a God, establishing
God by first principles. He also reasons on social
questions from first principles, and the procedure
whereby he establishes solutions for ethical and
social questions is the same as that by which he
proves the existence of God. God is the source
and fountainhead of all first principles and of
natural law. A formal system of obligations, gen-

eral and special virtues, and special authorities is then worked out. These are absolutized principles. The application of this system is productive of acute logic-chopping; its primary weakness is that it is absolutistic and supernatural, and refers material, natural, and social relationships to higher authorities; the result is a hierarchy of principles, duties, obligations, necessities.

One side of a critique of such a body of doctrine would refer to obligations in a feudal society, and has no reference to a bourgeois capitalist democracy. This is only one side, however—the genetic. It is presented today as the basis for contemporary solutions, and the method by which this hierarchy of relationships was established is advanced as the method for solving contemporary problems.[18] Hence, we must take this body of doctrine and examine it not merely in terms of its genesis, not merely in terms of its relation to feudal society, but also in reference to contemporary experience; examine what it means when it is applied today, as it is, directly and indirectly.

Thus, in his ethical teachings, Saint Thomas asks the question: *Are subjects bound to obey their*

[18] It should not be forgotten that the ideology defending contemporary Austrian Fascism has a Thomistic base, and that the Church supports Austrian Fascism materially as well as ideologically.

superiors in all things? There are, he finds, arguing from absolutized principles, two grounds on which subjects are not bound to obey their superiors in all things: One, if obedience would conflict with the command of a higher authority; the other, if the command is "given in a matter in which the receiver of the command is not subject." And here we find the introduction of the supernatural. There is the soul, and there is the body. A slave-owner can have no control over the soul of a slave, his authority being only over "what has to be done externally by the body." Here there is a qualification: "Man is not bound to obey man, but only God, in what belongs to the nature and physical being of the body, because in the physical order all men are equal, as touching the nourishment of the body and the begetting of offspring." Thus, obedience is not required in such matters as the contraction of marriage or the preservation of virginity. "But in the laying out of his day and the transaction of business, the subject is bound to obey his superior according to the character of his superiority . . . a slave his master in doing slave's work, a son his father in conduct of life and household management, and so of the rest."

We must examine the Thomistic method, then, not merely genetically but also in terms of its relevance to our times. We describe it as having a traditional influence that is still strong, but with a quite negligible carry-over value. Our fundamental criticism has to do with Aquinas' method and with its absolutizing of first principles. It is from this method and these first principles that he derives his formalized hierarchy of relationships and obligations; and it is through the utilization of this method and these principles that his followers today seek to establish, in our society, feudal relationships and feudal conceptions of obligation.

It may be remarked further that Aquinas is of interest to us today as an historical curiosity. And finally, if we are untainted by his dogma, and if we can successfully negate or destroy any active intellectual and social influence that stems from him, then we can say of his writings that they constitute a body of work furnishing us with objects of æsthetic contemplation and enjoyment, revealing to us yet one more effort of the human mind and spirit, one more system that is the product of a past society and the human brain, one more intellectual system that must be put into a glass case in the museum of philosophy.

Spinoza might here be juxtaposed with Aquinas. Spinoza and his writings belong to the traditional influence from our intellectual past. His God can be set in contrast to the God of Aquinas. Speaking of vengeance, Saint Thomas writes: "The secret judgments of God, whereby He temporally punishes some persons without fault of theirs, are not within the competence of human judgment to imitate; because man cannot comprehend the reasons of these judgments so as to know what is expedient for each individual soul." Contrast this with Spinoza's argument against the doctrine of God:

"If a stone falls from a roof on to someone's head and kills him, they will demonstrate by their new method that the stone fell in order to kill the man; for if it had not by God's will fallen with that object, how could so many circumstances . . . have all happened together by chance? Perhaps you will answer that the event is due to the facts that the wind was blowing, and the man was walking that way. 'But why,' they will insist, 'was the wind blowing, and why was the man at that very time walking that way?' . . . So they will pursue their questions from cause to cause, till at last you take refuge in the will of God—in other words, the sanctuary of ignorance."

Countering the argument of final causes, Spinoza said:

"Such persons [those who argue for final causes] know that, with the removal of ignorance, the wonder which forms their only available means for proving and preserving their authority would vanish also." [19]

Spinoza formulated a system of rational determinism. Redefining God's omnipotence, he reduced God to the status of a mathematical axiom, attacked attempts to endow God with human attributes such as intellect, and argued against "men lunatic enough to believe that even God himself takes pleasure in harmony." This side of Spinoza's system constituted, in its day, a forward and progressive step, and hence we can say that he rendered an incalculable service to the human race, for which he has justly earned undying fame. However, do we stop at the conclusion that Spinoza was on the side of life, and that therefore the philosopher of today should be on the side of life?

Obviously, we have here another problem facing us if we are to be critics of thought and philosophy, if we are concerned with assimilating and expressing and utilizing the best that man has thought and experienced. We must meet a more important question, must assess the carry-over

[19] This remark can most neatly be referred back to the appeal to authority which was made by the late Dr. Irving Babbitt and his disciples. It suggests the real nature of their argument and their appeal. Basically they have been "literary" philosophers, and behind this their appeal to authority was essentially a mask for ignorance of and prejudice against the modern world with its stresses and with the constantly new demands that it makes on man's intellect and powers of assimilation.

value and the intellectual utility of Spinoza in the modern world. Doing this, we find that a certain portion of Spinoza's thought is today sound and pertinent: part, for instance, of his rational formulation of determinism [20] freed from its theological trappings, and his attacks on superstition, his emphasis on testing knowledge by reference to experience, and many of his insights and definitions, such as his definition of wonder. Beyond these, what remains relevant today in Spinoza's thought? Before we can answer this we must think of *relevance* in a broader sense than that in which Mr. Hicks uses it in his effort to establish a standard of judgment for the historical novel. Rele-

[20] "Feuerbach asks: 'What does Spinoza mean when he speaks (logically or metaphysically) of substance and (theologically) of God?' . . . Feuerbach answers, categorically: 'Nothing else but nature.' . . . Spinoza has suppressed the dualism of God and nature, for he regards natural phenomena as the actions of God. But, for the very reason that in his view natural phenomena are the actions of God, God becomes for him a kind of being distinct from nature and one on which nature rests. God is for him subject, and nature is predicate. Philosophy, now that it has at length definitely emancipated itself from theological traditions, must rid itself of this grave defect in the Spinozist doctrine, sound though that doctrine is at bottom. . . . This Spinozism, freed from its theological lumber by Feuerbach, was the philosophy which Marx and Engels adopted when they broke away from idealism. But the freeing of Spinozism from its theological lumber implied the disclosure of the true materialist content of Spinoza's philosophy. Consequently, the Spinozism of Marx and Engels is materialism in its most modern form." Plekhanov, *op cit.*, pp. 10–11.

Plekhanov may here be exaggerating Spinoza's influence; but even if he is, I find some soundness in his contention.

vance is not merely relevance to the contemporary needs of the working class. It is relevance, rather, to *all* the problems of the modern world, both ideological and material; relevance in the sense in which we say that certain principles apply today as forcibly as they applied in Spinoza's time; relevance in that certain ideas suggestively lead us onward to a greater conquest of the world of ideas, and thus to the expansion of truth and knowledge.

Engels said that "the German working class is the inheritor of German classical philosophy." This may be broadened to mean that *the working class is the inheritor of the thought and the literature of the ages.* And unless we make this a pious platitude, we must go on to say that the way in which the working class is the inheritor of vital traditions and ideas is through *assimilation.* Now one of the tasks of criticism is the practice of judgment in assimilation. Unless this task be performed consciously, and with intelligence and imagination, there is great danger that critics may shift "the blame to the shoulders of others, to blame the masses of the workers for" their "own philistinism."

I have used contrasting analyses of Saint Thomas Aquinas and of Spinoza to illustrate the method that I think needs to be applied when we seek to consider and assimilate the valuable elements in the thought of the past. Those aspects of Spinoza's thought to which I have referred possess, I think, persistence-value. They are sound today. Their persistence-value has enabled them to carry over after they have been divorced from the society, the conditions and the basic set of material relationships out of which they developed. They are progressive rather than regressive influences, and—as such—are to be distinguished from, say, the regressive aspects of the thought and method of Thomas Aquinas.

The reasons and the relationships behind Spinoza's thought processes must interest us. However, in estimating the present value of his thought, we do not merely make a genetic analysis into these reasons and relationships. And an explanation, further, of these reasons and relationships does not prove, or disprove, the soundness of his ideas *per se*. It does not permit us to determine which part of his thought is alive now, and which part must now be regarded merely as an historical curiosity. We find that, in thought, there is also a relative objective validity, to be estimated in accordance with a broad and intelligent reference of ideas to our own knowledge, needs, and experiences.

74

And when we criticize the literature of the past, we do so in a method analogous to that which is here used summarily in my juxtaposition of Aquinas and Spinoza. If—and this remark bears emphatic repetition—we are to struggle toward sound and useful criticism, we do not merely emit the platitude that writers of the past wrote for their own times, and then paste on to this truism the platitude that modern writers must write for their own times.[21]

[21] "Great writers are generally born in the wombs of great crises: they reflect all the colorfulness and all the restless dynamics of the crisis, and the mainspring of their work is their anxiety to find some kind of consoling answer to the burning questions of life." Lunacharsky, quoted by Nathan Adler, in *Partisan Review, Number 2*.

I agree with this statement, though it is one that can be too easily distorted into a specious defense of complete contemporaneity and immediacy in literature. Also, it can be falsely used in an objective context, whereas its meaning is rather plainly subjective. The burning questions of life are not subtractible from their essential ideological framework. They never purely and solely exist on an economic basis. In addition, though in some ways they connect with fundamental points of economic and material origin, they are sometimes fought out almost completely on the ideological plane. Thus the question of the existence of God often becomes a "burning question of life" though not a purely economic question.

More important, if this remark be used to defend a theory of complete contemporaneity, it becomes self-defeating; for we cannot know what a "burning question of life" is, save for utter hunger and death. For a "burning question" today grows out of yesterday's conditions, and if we do not know those conditions, we also do not know many of the essentially causal aspects of that "burning question." Also, there is a difference between the subjective and the objective answers to any burning questions of the hour. A subjective answer, in the form of a regressive Christianity, may be very consoling though all that it gives is consolation in the face of the continuance of the question. An objective answer solves the problem, thereby eliminating the question. Dostoevski found a consoling answer through Christianity and the doctrine of the necessity of suffering, and thus is an example of Lunacharsky's thesis; but he did not find an objective answer. As frequently as not, an objective answer to a burning question does not bring consolation, because it requires a clear-eyed apprehension of truth and an effort to establish truth objectively.

Lunacharsky's statement cannot therefore be used as a rebuttal of my argument here. The present does not exist distinct from the past or the future. The past exists in the present, and even if we are not conscious of it, we are unconsciously affected by it, and in that case we are affected and driven by causes and conditions of which we are unaware. The failure to apprehend a cause does not eliminate that cause. Consolation and truth do not always walk hand-in-hand.

CHAPTER VIII

The Categories of "Bourgeois" and "Proletarian"

IF MY analysis and demonstration be acceptable, we are forced to the conclusion that some elements of the thought and the creative literature of the past survive, carrying with them some degree of æsthetic and objective validity. It is, then, safe to assume that some of the art and some of the thought of the present will retain elements of intellectual or æsthetic validity after the process of history and the passage of time have eliminated or solved the problems created by the conditions and the burning needs of our impermanent system of capitalist democracy.

Further, if this line of reasoning be correct, what becomes of the categories *bourgeois* and *proletarian* in their application to art, literature, and thought? These categories have often been applied confusingly. Thus they have been used in a descriptive sense on the one hand, and on the other they have been transferred from the status of descriptive standards to that of categories of value *per se*.

Michael Gold, with his usual Marxmanship, has given us one interesting application. Writing on Gilbert and Sullivan [22] he says that "when a Nazi with hands dripping with the blood of workers begins to sentimentalize over Wagner, or an ex-Czarist officer who has hung and flogged peasants, tells us that Dostoevsky shakes him to the very soul, one is perhaps justified in suspecting both Wagner and Dostoievsky," because "it is difficult to separate a work of art from the class out of which it has sprung and the audience it affects." Here the class status of the audience, even years after the artist is dead, is made a category; and from being a category it is tacitly shifted, by the very phrasing itself, into a qualitative judgment *per se*. Mr. Gold continues: "It [Gilbert and Sullivan's opera] is all the most glorious nonsense, and the music has a happy folk-dance quality. Nobody has ever written better popular music; it hasn't a single vulgar flaw. . . . I can testify to the hypnotic spell these two magicians cast upon me." Despite this effect, however, he remained worried, because "true class culture grows by . . . subcon-

[22] "The Gilbert-Sullivan Cult," *New Masses*, April 24, 1934.

scious accretion." And Gilbert, it must be remembered, was a Tory. And so, according to Mr. Gold,
"Such men are the 'cultural' pioneers of Fascism."
He therefore demands proletarian Gilbert-and-
Sullivan operas. Here the category *bourgeois* is
applied from a superficial recognition of the class-
consciousness of the audience, connected with the
subconscious and turned into an implicit judgment.

Granville Hicks [23] finds the bourgeois novel in-
completely satisfying. Contrary to Isidor Schneider
his adoption of a "Marxian" viewpoint has
changed his literary outlook. Thus, he presents
considerable detail to prove that he could not now
be so impressed by Proust as he once was. He confesses: "There is no bourgeois novel that, taken as
a whole, satisfies me. I am not merely conscious of
omission and irrelevancies; I feel within myself
a definite resistance, a counter-emotion, so to
speak, that makes a unified esthetic experience impossible." The present is, however, a period of
transition, and we have as yet no great proletarian
novels to substitute for great bourgeois novels.
Thus "the reason why revolutionary writers so
often seem clumsy is that they are trying to com-
municate the operation of what deserves to be

[23] "The Future of the Proletarian Novel"—final article in the series
"Revolution and the Novel," *New Masses*, May 22, 1934.

called a new type of sensibility." [24] In the future, they will achieve this expression in a socialist society. Until that society shall develop, "the integration toward which the revolutionary writer aims is limited by the outlook and needs of the proletariat. This means, obviously, an emphasis on class-consciousness and militancy, but the author most effectively creates such attitudes not by ignoring large sectors of life, but by integrating them with the class struggle."

Hicks spends considerable time discussing the themes about which a proletarian novelist might write; and he suggests that some themes, such as those dealing with the life of the petty bourgeoisie, will not generally satisfy the proletarian novelist. "The trouble is, of course, that such a theme does not give the author an opportunity to display the forces [the class-conscious vanguard of the proletariat and its leaders] that are working against the defeatism and incipient Fascism of the petty bourgeoisie." [25] Withal, Mr. Hicks does not impose restrictions on the proletarian novelist in

[24] *Ibid.*

[25] "Character and Classes" in the series "Revolution and the Novel," *New Masses*, April 24, 1934. In my opinion, the *greatest* American novel of our century is *An American Tragedy*. It may be considered as a case history of the American petty bourgeoisie. I wonder if many of our proletarian novelists would have been dissatisfied with such a theme if they had written *An American Tragedy*.

choice of themes and material. On the contrary, he is as broad as life, and even declares that the proletarian novelist may write about the past, the present, or the future. However, he thinks it most likely that the proletarian novelist, in writing about the past, will select a subject in which the feature of "relevance" is fairly obvious.[26] He mentions probable historical subjects that clearly would be classified here—Shays's Rebellion, the Paris Commune, and the French Revolution. He predicts a future in which the proletarian novel will surpass the bourgeois novel, and he pens a prophetic picture of the future proletarian novel:

"If we can imagine an author with Michael Gold's power of evoking scenes, and William Rollins' [27] structural skill, with Jack Conroy's wide acquaintance with the proletariat, with Louis Colman's [28] first-hand knowledge of the labor movement, with all the passion of these and a dozen other revolutionary novelists, with something of Dreiser's massive patience, we can see what shape a proletarian masterpiece might take. It would do justice to all the many-sided richness of the characters, exploring with Proustian persistence the deepest recesses of individuality and at the same time exhibiting that individuality as essentially a social phenomenon. And it

[26] *Ibid.*
[27] Author of *The Shadow Before.*
[28] Author of *Lumber.*

81

would carry its readers toward life, not, as *The Remem-brance of Things Past* does, toward death." [29]

Mr. Hicks here, as in *The Great Tradition*, re-veals a strong tendency to use the categories of bourgeois and proletarian literature as standards, and within them to judge works of literature in terms of themes and of formal ideology.

Often, when they have contrasted bourgeois and proletarian literature, revolutionary critics have been pressed into a dilemma. Bourgeois literature, so-called, has developed through a long tradition, and its heritage now includes a number of great works. Proletarian literature, so-called, has not had that same historical development. Revolutionary critics, proceeding in terms of these categories, have therefore been forced to counter what has been accomplished in bourgeois literature with faith in the prospects and potentialities of prole-tarian literature. Through many prognostications, much theorizing, countless prophecies, we have found these critics again and again cooking up recipes for tomorrow's "great" literature. Mr. Hicks' description of a future proletarian Proust, greater than Marcel Proust himself, is one of many such prophecies. These efforts suggest a remark of

[29] In *New Masses*, May 23, 1934.

Louis Grudin's. Speaking of the critic who applies standards of measurement instead of criteria of judgment, Mr. Grudin [30] comments: "His procedure has been that of an excursion for words and notions to support his claims, wherever he could find them; and he has had to trust to the meanings he could read into already available odds and ends belonging to various fields and gathered into a makeshift critical doctrine."

We can gain a further sense of the confusion in this aspect of the critical problem by considering the views of D. S. Mirsky on James Joyce. [31] After describing the social and ideological backgrounds and the personal history of Joyce, and proving that Joyce was introduced as a figure into the world of the international bourgeoisie by two millionaires, Mirsky asks the question whether or not Joyce offers any model for revolutionary writers:

"The answer is that his method is too inseparably connected with the specifically decadent phase of the bourgeois culture he reflects, is too narrowly confined within its limits. The use of the inner monologue (stream of consciousness method) is too closely connected with the ultra subjectivism of the parasitic, rentier bourgeoisie,

[30] Quoted by John Dewey in *Art as Experience*.
[31] "Joyce and Irish Literature," in the *New Masses*, April 3, 1934.

and entirely unadaptable to the art of one who is building socialist society. Not less foreign to the dynamics of
our [Russian] culture is the fundamentally static method
in which the picture of Bloom is composed. . . . There
remains still the most fundamental element of Joyce's
art, his realistic grasp, his amazing exactness of expression, all that side in which he is of the school of the
French naturalists, raising to its ultimate height their
cult of the *mot juste*. It is this exactness which gives
Joyce the wonderful realistic power in depicting the
outer world for which he is famous. But this has its roots
on the one hand in a morbid, defeatist delight in the
ugly and repulsive and, on the other, in an aesthetico-
proprietary desire for the possession of 'things'. So that
even this one realistic element of Joyce's style is fundamentally foreign to the realism towards which Soviet art
aims, mainly a mastery of the world by means of active,
dynamic materialism—with the purpose of not merely
understanding but also changing the reality of history." [32]

These quotations reveal the widespread confusion that has accompanied the applications of such
categories to literature. Mirsky assumes such a direct tie-up between economics and literature that
he finds Joyce's exactitude in description to be an
acquisitive and an æsthetico-proprietary desire for

[32] Mirsky's remarks on Joyce might be contrasted with Edmund Wil-
son's analysis in *Axel's Castle*.

"things"; and that Joyce's utilization of the interior monologue is too closely connected with a parasitic element of the bourgeoisie to be usable by revolutionary writers. Such discoveries enable Mirsky to legislate for writers at wholesale on what will or will not influence them.

Michael Gold, seeking to apply these categories, extends them to the audience, applies them retroactively to dead authors, and calls upon the subconscious for abetment in his damnation of bourgeois art. And Granville Hicks, in order to establish the importance of proletarian literature, even relies on such badly subjective evidence as the flat statement that no bourgeois novel will provide him with a unified æsthetic experience. The proper duties of criticism are ignored, and the carry-over value of literature is almost completely disregarded. Functional extremism rampantly leads to one-sided formulæ, the rationalization of prejudices, and the concoction of meaningless recipes for the novelist of the classless society of the future.

Here it becomes necessary to re-emphasize a fairly apparent fact. The "bourgeois" novel has had a long history. It is possible to examine that history, to note the various types of novel that are included within the category, to arrive at some fairly accurate definitions, and even to make some fairly accurate descriptions of its growth and its methods. But with "proletarian" literature this cannot be done, because that literature is now only at the beginning of its history. It will grow and develop as part of the development of literature in general. It will not grow from the definitions of critics. In its growth it will—for some time to come—be constantly influenced by "bourgeois" literature. The assimilation will not be even and regular; it will not proceed according to the dictates of critical legislation. And since literature is a qualitative matter, and since it is æsthetic and subjective as well as functional and objective, the growth of future proletarian literature will not *per se* prove the failure of Joyce or Proust, let alone the failure of Dreiser or Melville. A proletarian classic in the future will not necessarily give rise to dispraise of *Ulysses,* any more than *Macbeth* can logically be cited in dispraise of Dante's *Divine Comedy*, or than Milton's *Paradise Lost* can be used to prove the failure of the author of *Beowulf*.

§ 2

It seems to me that there are the following possible definitions of proletarian literature: it can be defined as creative literature written by a member of the industrial proletariat, regardless of the author's political orientation; as creative literature that reveals some phase of the experience of the industrial proletariat, regardless of the political orientation of the author; as creative literature written by a member of the industrial proletariat who is class-conscious in the Marxian sense, and a member of the proletarian vanguard; as creative literature written by a class-conscious member of the proletariat and treating solely (or principally) of some phase of the life of that group; as creative literature written about that group within the proletariat regardless of the author's class status or his group status within his class; as creative literature written in order to enforce, through its conclusions and implications, the views of the proletarian vanguard; as creative literature read by the proletariat; as creative literature read by the proletarian vanguard; or as creative literature combining these features in differing combinations.

Irrespective of which of these definitions or combination of definitions one applies, it remains that they do not *per se* constitute a category of value. They do not constitute an *a priori* fiat for the critical destruction of works that will not slide into such a category. Moreover, it does not follow that works of literature snugly fitting into whichever of these definitions (or combinations of definitions) one adopts will be uninfluenced by literature that is unqualifiedly non-proletarian, like Proust's works, or unqualifiedly non-revolutionary, in the political sense, like T. S. Eliot's. For there is a continuity in literature and literary influences, just as there is in thought and in science. The literary process continues whether or not we are critically conscious of it. The tightening of categories into absolutes does not destroy this continuity; it merely diverts the literary influences into a subterranean channel. In so doing, it does not subject them to the test of sensible and intelligent critical evaluation. And this is precisely the error that "leftism" has committed in its effort to harden categories and to ignore the carry-over value in literature.

Since literature is not made by definitions of categories, the definition of proletarian literature presented by our revolutionary critics is not, objectively, so important as they assume it to be. The establishment of functional categories sets up standards of measurement rather than criteria of judgment. But—as is pertinently suggested by John Dewey in *Art as Experience*—it is criteria of judgment, not standards of measurement, that are the business of criticism. And the overemphasis of definitions and categories is least relevant when it is referred to a trend in literature that is only at the beginning of its history, only now preparing to spread its wings and fly in many directions.

Any revolutionary critic who would defend himself against my analysis, and argue that the categories of bourgeois and proletarian are more than descriptive, must take one of two positions: he must admit and adopt a double standard, a dual set of criteria, or else he must favor the destruction of one at the expense of the other. If he recognizes two different sets of criteria—one for proletarian values and proletarian literature, and another for bourgeois values and bourgeois literature—he is contradicting his own position, and consistency will demand that he make adjustments of it elsewhere. He sets a wall between bourgeois values and proletarian values in literature. Not advocating the destruction of bourgeois values, he can then grant them a right to existence only as bourgeois values. For him, this position is utterly untenable; he has only one resource—and that is to recognize that these categories are descriptive.

If he adopts the other position, advocating the destruction of bourgeois values and bourgeois influences, and the creation, enlargement, and solidification of proletarian values and proletarian influences, he must answer certain questions. Where is he to find the source from which he will develop his strictly proletarian values? The answer is—in the life and the needs of the proletariat. But the proletariat does not exist in total isolation from the bourgeoisie, nor from bourgeois influences; it does not, for one thing, live free from tradition.[33] And so, despite the critics' sternest defense, bourgeois

[33] In *What Is to Be Done?* Lenin writes: "Since there can be no talk of an independent ideology being developed by the masses of the workers in the process of their movement, then *the only choice is:* Either bourgeois or Socialist ideology. There is no middle course (for humanity has not created a third ideology, and moreover, in a society torn by class antagonism there can never be a non-class or above class ideology)." And in a footnote he adds: "This does not mean, of course, that the workers have no part in creating such an ideology. But they take part not as workers, but as Socialist theoreticians . . . in other words, they take part only to the extent that they are able, more or less, to acquire the knowledge of their age and advance that knowledge. And in order that working men *may be able to do this more often,* efforts must be made to raise the level of the consciousness of the workers generally; care must be taken that the workers do not confine themselves to the artificially restricted limits of *literature for workers* but that they study *general literature* to an increasing degree. It would even be more true to say, 'were not confined', instead of 'not confine themselves', because the workers themselves wish to read and do read all that is written for the intelligentsia and it is only a few (bad) intellectuals who believe that it is sufficient 'for the workers' to tell them a few things about factory conditions, and to repeat over and over again what has long been known."

If the knowledge of an age must be mastered, what is the source of most of that knowledge? Obviously, in our age, it is bourgeois. If there can only be either a bourgeois or a Socialist ideology, what is the inference? Obviously, that that knowledge, so far as it has value, must be assimilated into socialist ideology, and used as the basis for advancing the knowledge of the age. Is not the same thing, then, true of culture in general? I contend that it is.

values will be smuggled in. If barbed-wire fences are to be placed around the minds of the proletariat and its allies, what then of the stream of cultural continuity? If the critic would like to dam off this stream of cultural continuity, does he actually believe that he can? Yet it seems to me that a relentless enforcement of the view that the categories "bourgeois" and "proletarian" are disconnectably separable, that they are standards, and that the proletariat has all of its values created within the range of its own class experience, leads inevitably to that conclusion. For to say that bourgeois values are useless to the proletariat in culture, to say that proletarian values will take their place uninfluenced by bourgeois values, is to contend that the cultural values and achievements that have grown out of the past are useless to the proletariat, and must therefore be destroyed. But a relentlessly enforced leftist theory leads logically to this conclusion, and to follow it out in action and in criticism constitutes an effort toward such an achievement—if achievement it can be called. The critic who is faced with this interpretation will deny it. Yet what other conclusion can be drawn from his reasoning?

Obviously, this view was not held by the great revolutionary Marxist leaders. Further, it is a position that is today rapidly losing ground in America; though, because at one time it did exert a stronger influence on the revolutionary movement, remnants of it are still to be encountered. Such a theory is not one that preserves culture, for culture permits a more, rather than a less, conscious assimilation of the cultural heritage— which was the aim of all the great Marxist leaders.

André Gide has written: [34]

"In every enduring work of art . . . one that is capable of appealing to the appetites of successive generations, there is to be found a good deal more than a mere response to the momentary needs of a class or a period. It goes without saying that it is a good thing to encourage the reading of such masterpieces; and the U.S.S.R., by its reprints of Pushkin and its performances of Shakespeare, better shows its real love of culture than it does by the publication of a swarm of productions which, while they may be remarkable enough in kind, and while they may exalt its triumphs, are possessed, possibly, of but a passing interest. The mistake, I feel, lies in trying to indicate too narrowly, too precisely, just what is to be looked for in the great works of the past, the lesson that is to be learned from them."

When one freezes the categories of bourgeois and

[34] In a paper read before the First International Congress of Writers for the Defense of Culture, held in Paris in the summer of 1935. Printed in the *Partisan Review*, No. 9, translated by Samuel Putnam.

proletarian and insists that they be standards of measurement in literature, one shuts out the enduring element that Gide speaks of. This is, baldly, the position of leftism when it uses its categories in such a way. And it does not sponsor a method that preserves culture. It should remain, then, that the categories bourgeois and proletarian, when applied to literary criticism, are not the basis of value judgment *per se;* rather, they are descriptive categories. Within the category bourgeois, there will be found both progressive and regressive elements. One of the fundamental duties of revolutionary criticism is, as I have already suggested in my comments on Aquinas and Spinoza, to assimilate and further the understanding of the progressive elements, and to negate the influence of the regressive ones.[35] By performing such a task, which is his

[35] Marx in *The Poverty of Philosophy* criticizes Proudhon for assuming that "every economic category has two sides, the one good, the other bad. . . . The *good* and the *bad* side, the *advantage* and the *inconvenience,* taken together, form for M. Proudhon the contradiction in each economic category. The problem to solve: To conserve the good side while eliminating the bad." Slavery is cited as an example. "What will M. Proudhon do to save slavery? He puts the problem: Conserve the good side of this economic category, eliminate the bad." Marx then shows that Proudhon is here arbitrary. "It is not the category which poses and opposes itself by its contradictory nature, it is M. Proudhon who disturbs himself, argues with himself, strives and struggles between the two sides of the category. . . . He takes the first category to hand and arbitrarily attributes to it the quality of becoming a remedy to the inconveniences of the category which he wishes to purify. . . In thus taking successively the economic categories one by one and making one

legitimate one, the critic does not dam up the stream of cultural continuity. Furthermore, his task—evaluating the literature of the present—is not simply and solely that of putting it into categories; nor that of legislating themes on the basis of such categories; nor that of grandiloquently describing future proletarian Prousts greater than Proust. It is rather the task of understanding, assimilating, evaluating, interpreting the literature of the present in a manner analogous to that in which he treats the literature of the past. And if he meets these obligations with intelligence and imagination, he is contributing toward the assimilation of cultural influences and cultural values.

---

the antidote of the other, M. Proudhon makes of this mixture of contradictions and of antidotes to contradictions, two volumes of contradictions which he calls by their proper title: 'The System of Economic Contradictions'." (Pp. 121, 123.)

I quote this in order to make the point that I am not speaking here of such categories; I am dealing with larger ones. Also, I am not speaking of "good" and "bad" categories within these categories. I am speaking of "the succession of ideas" (the phrase is Marx's) and of the succession of cultural values.

CHAPTER IX

Individualism and the Class Struggle

A GENERALIZED description of one of the rôles played by literature is that it is a record of how people feel at different times. John Strachey in *The Coming Struggle for Power* (Covici-Friede) writes: " 'Literature' is perhaps the most remarkable of all the ideal constructions which the human mind has begotten. It is a great sea into which for centuries have been poured all those thoughts, dreams, fantasies, concepts, ascertained facts, and emotions, which did not fit into any of the other categories of human thought. Into literature have gone philosophical ideas too tenuous for the philosophers, dreams too literal for plastic expression, ascertained facts too uncorrelated for science, and emotions too intertwined with the particular instance to find expression in the glorious and precise abstractions of music."

It is characteristic of life that it constantly tends

to overflow the intellectual categories which are set up as the basis for apprehending, organizing, understanding, controlling and changing it. Strachey's definition here is an elaboration of the rôle that literature plays as a reservoir for this overflow.

Strachey goes on thus: "Literature, for the most part, attempts to illuminate some particular predicament of a particular man or a particular woman at a given time and place." Literature, in this aspect, can conceivably permit a great diversity in method, in procedure, and in content. Time was when "leftist" critics tended to deny such a variety; but they are now ready to grant it, at least as a possibility. Granville Hicks in *The Great Tradition* (Macmillan, revised edition, International Publishers) says that revolutionary literature can have diversity. He speaks of "the most important differences of all, the differences that are inherent in the nature of revolutionary literature. If all bourgeois survivals could be miraculously obliterated, and if the same high talent everywhere prevailed, monotony would by no means be the result."

However much this variety may be granted in a general statement, it has not been sufficiently revealed in specific literary criticism, in reviews, and in editorial policies. A kind of self-consciousness

on the part of writers persists as a hangover from
the days when leftists strove to legislate themes
and subject matter; often an admirer of a book,
in reviewing it, would be required to emphasize
that even though it contained no strike scenes or
demonstrations, it was nevertheless revolutionary
—or, at least, a valuable piece of "exposure" literature. Similarly, again and again, there have been
book reviews complaining that the author of a
particular book was all right as far as he had gone,
but that he had not gone far enough. And recently,
Clifford Odets,[36] arguing in defense of propaganda, declared that propagandists do not "ex-
cuse" James Joyce for "his *bad* themes."

Dealing with James Joyce,[37] Karl Radek has revealed a similar tendency, and I think that it is
worth our while to present and analyze his judgment. Radek contends that "it does not lie within
the power of bourgeois art to imitate the realism
of Balzac, who endeavored to paint a picture com-
mensurate with the epoch in which he lived. For
a full picture of life as it is would be a condemna-

---

[36] "All Drama Is Propaganda," in *Controversy*, February, 1936.
[37] *James Joyce, or Socialist Realism*, from *Contemporary World Literature and the Tasks of the Proletariat*, a report delivered at the Congress of Soviet Writers, August, 1934. Pp. 151–4. See also *Problems of
Soviet Literature*, by A. Zhdanov, Maxim Gorky, N. Bukharin, K. Radek,
A. Stetsky. International Publishers.

tion of moribund capitalism." [38] He goes on to cite
Joyce as an example. "His basic feature is the conviction that there is nothing big in life—no big

[38] Naturalism in literature was an attempt to utilize scientific method
in the novel. It worked more or less on the theory that character is
the product of environment. The first developments in such a direction
would, by the very nature of environment, treat of environment and
the relationship of environment to character. The first works of naturalism would more or less have to be extensive rather than intensive.
Also, naturalism was tied to the development of materialism. The earlier
materialism was mechanistic, and so environment was juxtaposed to
character.

This is important in the development of naturalism as a method and
an influence in literature. Naturalism as a method would have to go on,
and develop various implications. Likewise, it would have to reveal a
growing and changing method. The shift of emphasis from the extensive
to the intensive was, as a consequence, a somewhat necessary and understandable development. If the world is a process, and the factor of
change is a noticeable characteristic of the world as process, then the
attempt to embody the world as process would become intertwined with
naturalism. Two developments would flow out of the potentialities of
naturalism. One would be a shift in emphasis to a more intensive method,
and an attempt to embody precision of details and the like over a small
area. This we find in Joyce. The other would be an attempt to apply
the conception of the world as process to the individual consciousness,
and this would result in psychological relativism. This we find in Proust
and Joyce.

A literary method and tradition in time reacts on itself. It leads
to the development of various potentialities wrapped within whatever
fundamental assumptions it possesses either implicitly or explicitly. These
fundamental assumptions would not be directly the product of economics
and the base of a society. They would be the products of that, connected
with ideological strains of development, reacting to form the basis for
a view that would lead to the beginnings of a literary method and a
tradition; and in addition, there would be intertwined with it past
literary methods and traditions.

Radek here tends to leave out links in the relationship, and thus
arrives at an interpretation which I consider too simplified, and therefore, too schematized.

events, no big people, no big ideas; and the writer can give a picture of life by just taking 'any given hero on any given day' and reproducing him with exactitude. A heap of dung, crawling with worms, photographed by a cinema apparatus through a microscope—such is Joyce's work. . . . The picture that he gives . . . does not fit even those trivial heroes in that trivial life which he depicts. The scene of his book is laid in Ireland in 1916.[39] The petty bourgeois whom he describes are Irish types, though laying claim to universal human significance. But these Blooms and Daedaluses, whom the author relentlessly pursues into the lavatory, the brothel and the pothouse, did not cease to be petty bourgeois when they took part in the Irish insurrection of 1916. The petty bourgeois is a profoundly contradictory phenomenon; and in order to give a portrayal of the petty bourgeois, one must present him in all his relations to life. Joyce . . . has selected a piece of life and depicted that. His choice is determined by the fact that for him the whole world lies between a cupboardful of medieval books, a brothel and a pothouse. For him, the national revolutionary movement of the Irish petty bourgeoisie does not exist; and consequently

[39] This is an error of fact. The story is laid in June, 1904.

99

the picture which he presents, despite its ostensible impartiality, is untrue."

Radek then concludes, among other things, that Joyce's method is unsatisfactory for the presentation of themes of class struggle; Balzac and Tolstoy are more appropriate models for the Soviet writers. In rebuttal of disagreements with his interpretation, Karl Radek says: "All that appealed to Joyce was the medieval, the mystical, the reactionary in the petty bourgeoisie—lust, aberrations; everything capable of impelling the petty bourgeoisie to join the side of revolution was alien to him." [40]

The basis of this criticism is, I think, that Joyce failed to write what Radek, retroactively, desires him to have written. Radek is applying not criteria of judgment but standards of measurement; these standards of measurement relate to class phenomena, and he is proving Joyce a bourgeois writer and then condemning him because he is not the kind of bourgeois writer that Balzac was. Radek applies the standard that a writer must treat the whole of the life of his characters. But Joyce did not treat the whole of the life of the petty bour-

[40] Karl Radek praises Dostoevski, to whom these same aspects appealed. Dostoevski consciously affirmed even the mystical and the reactionary; and the phenomena of aberration are curiously important in his writings.

geoisie. No writer can succeed in presenting all of
life nor all of one class in a book or even in many
books. A writer does not surmount all the limitations of his time, his heritage, and many other hu-
manly and socially qualifying factors and conditions. Radek's criticism is of a type that is irrelevant
and unreasonable.

One of the ideological and social backgrounds
of Joyce's work is Irish nationalism, to which we
find him antagonistic. His revulsion goes back to
the Parnell episode, which shook Irish history and
bitterly split the Irish nation. Instead of condemning Joyce, however, it would be more fruitful for
us to investigate this antagonism as it is refracted
through his work, by making a genetic approach
to its sources. Such an approach would provide us
with an emotional awareness of this feature of Irish
life; and it would furnish us with much illustrative information.

A second ideological source in Joyce is Roman
Catholicism, which connects closely with Irish nationalism. Ireland is a Church-ridden country, and
the clergy played an important—and infamous—
rôle in the Parnell case. Ireland is strongly Catholic,
belligerently Catholic, furiously Catholic; and,
whether or not the reactionary elements of the
petty bourgeoisie appealed to Joyce, his attack on

Catholicism in Ireland has banned his works from his own country and made him a pariah.

Has a Marxist, then, any right to take a position like Karl Radek's on Joyce? Is a Marxist warranted in judging from so philistine a viewpoint while failing to consider the relation of Irish Catholicism and nationalism to Joyce's work?

Finally, the relation of Joyce to Irish literature must be considered; there we find him among the first to utilize the urban life of Ireland as the material for Irish writing. In the main, his predecessors utilized material from native folklore, from the life of the peasantry, and the like. This fact was a tremendous step forward in the history of Irish literature. All such factors are ignored by Radek in order to enforce a blanket condemnation.

The Irish revolution and civil war have both been given extensive treatment in Irish literature. I might cite the following works: *The Clanking of Chains*, by Brinsley Macnamara; *Juno and the Paycock, The Shadow of a Gunman*, and *The Plough and the Stars*, by Sean O'Casey; *The Informer* and *The Martyr*, by Liam O'Flaherty; *Guests of the Nation*, by Frank O'Connor; *Midsummer Night Dream* and *A Nest of Simple Folk* by Sean O'Faolin. None of these writers, be it noted, attempts to describe all of the life of Ireland. They utilize some of its features, and some aspects of the life of the petty bourgeoisie; and their works relate to the national revolutionary movement and the civil war. These works, along with *Ulysses*, refract a sense of Irish life. In some of these works (such as *The Clanking of Chains*, and also a much more effective novel of Macnamara's, *The Valley of the Squinting Windows*) we find a revulsion from Irish life as strong and as intense as it is in *Ulysses*. Does this not suggest to us that here are the phenomena of Irish life refracted through Irish literature, and that the picture warrants our investigation? In literature as well as in politics, local peculiarities find any number of expressions and reflections, and these must be considered when one indulges in literary criticism. All such features are ignored in Radek's criticism of Joyce, and in consequence we get a one-sided view. And further, there is the fact that Joyce has influenced several writers who have to some extent treated the national revolutionary movement; and it is not unsafe to prophesy that, when and if a novel dealing with the revolutionary movement in Ireland is written so as to satisfy Mr. Radek's thesis of socialist realism,[42] it will be shown to have been

---

[42] The basis for Karl Radek's criticism of Joyce is the thesis of socialist realism. Radek's definition is: "Realism means giving a picture not only

of the decay of capitalism and the withering away of its culture, but also of the birth of that class, of that force, which is capable of creating a new society and a new culture. . . . But there is no such thing as static realism. . . . Socialist realism means not only knowing reality as it is, but knowing whither it is moving. It is moving toward socialism, it is moving toward the victory of the international proletariat. And a work of art created by a socialist realist is one which shows whither that conflict of contradictions is leading which the artist has seen in life and reflected in his work."

Bukharin (also in *Problems of Soviet Literature,* pp. 150–3) says of socialist realism: "Its philosophical basis is dialectical materialism. . . . If socialist realism is distinguished by its active, operative character; if it does not give just a dry photograph of a process; if it projects the entire world of passion and struggle into the future; if it raises the heroic principle to the throne of history—then revolutionary romanticism is a component part of it." In *American Writers' Congress,* Edwin Seaver, in his definition of the proletarian novel in his paper presents practically the same thesis.

I understand Socialist realism to be a reaction against leftist tendencies such as those sponsored some years back by the now-dissolved RAPP. Those who argue for a "line" of "Socialist realism" do not bar the assimilation of past cultural values, and therefore cannot be said to treat the categories *bourgeois* and *proletarian* as categories of value alone. They see two tendencies dialectically operating in the world: moribund capitalism, which is on the decline; and socialism which is on the rise. The cultural assimilation they would accept is not an assimilation from the present—when capitalism is dying, but from the past, when the middle class was a progressive force. For instance, in literature they emphasize such writers as Shakespeare, Pushkin, Tolstoy, and Balzac.

Taking Edwin Seaver, in America, as a definite exponent of this line, we see that the emphasis is not purely mechanical, locking out "extra"- proletarian achievements in literature. Seaver defended Henry Roth's excellent first novel, *Call It Sleep,* which could not be put into any narrow leftist classification of revolutionary literature. More recently, he has praised *The Last Puritan* by Santayana, the ideologue *par excellence* of the escapist way of life. Praising Santayana, Seaver could not consistently attack the proposition that the categories *bourgeois* and *proletarian* are descriptive.

Besides being an attack on leftism, socialist realism represents a vital and healthy tendency. Still, it has not freed itself of the vice of functional extremism. Radek's criticism of Joyce shows us that vice in a naked light. He measures Joyce by extra-literary standards, mixing essential and non-essential references in order to treat Joyce in purely ideological terms. What is essentially unsound in Radek's criticism is, I think, his failure properly to apply a concept of necessity in literary judgment, and—consonantly—his inability to make essential rather than non-essential references from Joyce's work to its ideological and social backgrounds. I shall deal with the concept of necessity in a future chapter.

A principal criticism of the "line" of socialist realism is that it seems to be developing a literary eschatology in advance of the development of the literature itself. It presents not only a directive emphasis but also definitions, and these become standards. The standards are used as external measurements. The work of literature is then measured to fit the standards, and the result is extra-literary criticism.

The reasoning presented in exposition and defense of a "line" of socialist realism simplifies processes. It skips several phases of inter-relationships in the literary process, and in the connection of that process with others. Literature reacts on itself. In reacting upon itself, it reveals many streams of influence and counter-influence. Insufficiently apprehending the myriad reactions of literature upon itself, the proponents of socialist realism simplify literary influences. An example is Radek's argument that Balzac would be a healthier influence on Soviet writers than Joyce, because Balzac wrote at a time when the middle class was healthy, and Joyce writes of the middle class at an opposite historical pole. To arrive at such a simplified formulation, Radek merely skips seventy-five or a hundred years of literary development and of the reactions of literature upon itself.

Such simplifications lead him and other champions of this "line" to give writers wholesale advice on how they can and should be influenced. They also make the false assumption that literary masters are always the best influences for a writer—which is not necessarily correct. There are literary masters whose work will have eternal charm for a writer. There are masterpieces which a writer will recognize as such, without being importantly influenced by them. And there are various types of literary influences—technical, psychological, ideological, stimulating, suggestive. Critics like Radek ignore these matters.

Bukharin shows a greater interest in internal literary influences than does Radek. However, there is in his thinking a tendency toward mechanical application, noticeable in his *Historical Materialism,* where he treats philosophical and social thought: In his analysis of literature (from *Problems of Soviet Literature*) traces of this same mechanical approach are to be seen. Thus, his synthesizing of romanticism and realism as component parts of socialist realism is mechanical and formal. Here he influenced—most likely profitably—by Joyce's *Ulysses*.[43]

simplifies two literary movements in order to establish a thesis and an antithesis. An easy if irrelevant dialectical exercise is then permitted, and a wish-fulfillment is produced.

His paper is suave, showing broad culture and wide sources of information. But he utilizes these advantages in such a way that they tend to lose some of their impressiveness. He also arrives at definitions for writing in advance of the very writing that is defined. There is no inherent objection to this practice. Its relevance here is merely dubious. The first talented writer who appears will probably disregard these definitions, but they will probably persist and be applied to his own work. There is likely to be a tendency to judge work from preconceptions of dubious relevance.

We can, then, repeat that the *tendency in literature* which socialist realism prognosticates as a thesis is vital. But it will lead to the creation of literature; the *definitions* will not, nor will the *preconceptions* which are used for the formulation of its theses. When and as this literature is developed and expanded, it will have to be judged qualitatively. The tendency here is to judge quantitatively.

The formulation of this line has also resulted in predictions. To quote Radek: "We will create a literature higher than that of the Renaissance, for it derived its models from slave-owning Greece and slave-owning Rome and expressed the interests of rising capitalism, while our literature reflects the idea of a new, socialist society." It is not a defense of either capitalism or slavery to say that this is a *non-sequitur*. Different kinds of literature develop in different circumstances and different societies. Certain kinds of writing—Proust's, for instance—can come only at the end of a period; these have that peculiar beauty that is seen in decay. To make this recognition means, I think, neither to be an escapist nor to foster decay as decay. It is rather the recognition of the manner in which social conditions and the like are refracted through literature.

The question here is not that of creating, by prediction, a literature higher than any other literature. It is a case of keeping alive the stream of living literature; adding to it and working for the understanding of it. We must distinguish between the actual drive toward, and production of, revolutionary writing, and some of the contentions of those who seek to predict its course. These prophets are threatening to produce a new revolutionary "classicism" and to make of it an external standard.

[43] For a statement agreeing with Radek's interpretation of Joyce, see

§ 2

Strachey's definition of literature, quoted earlier in this chapter, obviously inclines toward writing that is "individualistic" rather than "collective." It recalls the time recently when there was a tendency to bifurcate the novel into the individualistic and the collective. Such a bifurcation produced the invention of notions. Individualism, as a concept carried into literature, is uncertain in its meaning. It seems largely to have been taken out of its context in the theories of classical economy. In its reference to laissez-faire economy, it has attained a justly merited unpopularity; for it embodies the theory that the individual is the best judge of his own interests and needs and wants, and that he is entitled to satisfy them in his own way, with a minimum of restraint.

While this theory may seem harmless when it is so stated, it is a basic assumption on which our system of "rugged individualism" is built. Not

Edwin Seaver's review of *Problems of Soviet Literature* in *New Masses*, Oct. 22, 1935. Mr. Seaver writes: "I remember, when first reading the abbreviated report of Karl Radek's address on contemporary world literature, resenting his attack on James Joyce as the antithesis of socialist realism. I must admit, however, that a closer examination of Radek's speech, and especially his answer to the discussion which followed, reveals a cogency of argument that is pretty hard to refute."

only the word, but its unpopularity in this economic theory, has been on occasion smuggled into literary criticism. I have already quoted Mirsky's statement that Joyce's exactness in describing objects reveals an "æsthetico-proprietary interest in things." This is only one example of many misapplications in transferring the concepts of individualism or the word itself from economic theory into literary criticism. It is true that Mirsky's comment applies to certain kinds of books, and if the *ci-devant* "Prince" Mirsky had only read these, he would have been able to judge more accurately. Thus one can say that in some of Joseph Hergesheimer's novels the descriptions of objects suggest a proprietary, even a leisure-class, interest in "things"; but even so, the criticism touches on what is only a minor aspect of his work. And the novels of Margaret Ayer Barnes read somewhat like treatises on upholstery.

Even in novels that have taken the individualistic viewpoint of the young man against the world, the writers have always had the world there, standing against the young man. Floyd Dell's Moon Calf, the hero of Somerset Maugham's *Of Human Bondage*, Stephen Daedalus—to take three novels from different countries and on different levels of ability and accomplishment—all these had to deal with the world. Often novelists have been unsound theoretically, and have consequently assumed that the individual stands alone, that he possesses free will, that he is the master of his fate, the captain of his soul; though even in those cases he has not been free from the influence of social pressures and forces. So that in saying that such novels are individualistic we must qualify to the effect that their authors have worked with an unsound theme and theory, and that in many cases the whole course of the narrative has contradicted their individualistic emphasis.

I discuss these questions at some length, because we often find them to have been the starting points of a bifurcation into the "individualistic" and the "collective" novel. A revolutionary critic generally demands of a novelist that he reveal the working of social forces (classes) and of social influences in a novel. However, social forces do not work like huge contrasting lumps pushed one against the other, and the treatment of them as such is a fallback to the materialism that preceded Marx. Social forces (classes) are the basis upon which societies are built. From them, institutions are developed; on them the ideological superstructure is built. Connected with the ideological superstructure is tradition related into the play of class forces, and into the ideology that directly connects the class forces at a given time. All these forces and influences work through the consciousness of men; sometimes through their unconsciousness. Ideology develops the appearance of independence. Here we must remember that "once an historic element has been brought into the world by other elements, *ultimately* by economic facts, it also reacts in its turn and may react on its environment and even on its own causes." [44] (Italics mine.) We must here distinguish between social forces, which, basically, are social classes, and social influences, which constitute all manner of ideological elements, connecting, interconnecting, reacting upon each other and back upon the base. We cannot then treat social forces as mechanical, and "the basis of this is the common undialectical conception of cause and effect as rigidly opposite poles." [45]

Therefore, because a novel happens to deal with the particular predicament of a particular man or woman in a particular period of time, it does not necessarily follow that it is tainted with individualism; nor—because it is "tainted" with "individualism"—does it necessarily follow that it

[44] *Marx-Engels, Selected Correspondence*, No. 227—Engels & Mehring, London, 14 July, 1893.
[45] *Ibid.*, p. 312.

belongs in a lower category than the collective novel; nor is it necessarily implied that the novelist has failed to understand the working of social forces and social influences; nor does it demand the conclusion that the masses will not read the book; nor, finally, that *ipso facto* it reveals such tendencies in the novelist himself as an "æsthetico-proprietary interest in things."

Granville Hicks [46] suggests a distinction between the "collective" and the "complex" novel. His suggestion here is formal, however, like most of the comments in his series on "Revolution and the Novel"; thus his distinctions seem to have little meaning for the novelist, the critic, or the reader. All that his series seems to have accomplished is the construction of pigeonholes: the novel of the past, the present, and the future; the biographical and the dramatic novel; the novel that is collective; and the novel that is complex. When writers begin to wonder whether they will write a collective or a complex novel, a biographical or a dramatic novel, they might as well leave off writing and hunt another job.[47] Likewise, when critics occupy their

---

[46] *The Great Tradition.* Also, *New Masses*, April 10, 1934.

[47] "In . . . *Revolution and the Novel* . . . Granville Hicks has probed these problems in fiction. However, though Hicks has helped to clarify our approach, his method of classifying unimportant details, as well as his choice of critical subjects, is removed from the way the writer faces

time in the building of pigeonholes, they suggest
that they are rapidly approaching the point where
they have outlived their critical usefulness. At all
events, I suspect a note of apology in Hicks' references to the treatment of individuals in the novel.
Thus the confession: "We do not know what kind
of novels will be written in the classless society,
but it is already clear that, during the long period
of transition, many though not all revolutionary
writers will be concerned in their work with individuals." [48]

Actually, there is nothing astounding in the fact
that novelists are likely to go on writing about individuals, because, after all, the world is made up
of individual human beings, and as Engels wrote:
"Everything which sets men in motion must go
through their minds; but what form it will take
in the mind will depend very much upon the circumstances." [49]

---

these problems. The writer does not decide *a priori* whether he will
write a dramatic or complex novel; his choice is determined by a number of psychological and thematic factors. In general Hicks has given
us a class analysis of the more obvious elements in fiction without first
establishing essential Marxian generalizations about the relation of method
to theme and form in terms of expanding audiences and new standards."
William Phillips and Philip Rahv in *Recent Problems of Revolutionary
Literature*, in *Proletarian Literature in the United States*. Edited by
Granville Hicks, Michael Gold, Isidor Schneider, Joseph North, Paul
Peters, Alan Calmer. P. 71. (International Publishers).
[48] *New Masses*, April 10, 1934.
[49] *Ludwig Feuerbach*, p. 60.

To continue, then, Mr. Hicks in dealing with the collective novel says that the "problem of creating credible individuals without destroying the sense of group unity is the great problem of the collective novel." [50] This, I presume, is to be classified as a household hint to novelists; though what Mr. Hicks probably means is that you can portray individuals in a collective novel. He bases his distinction between the collective and the complex novel on the ground that the collective novel deals with a group as a group, while the complex novel deals with a number of persons rather than with one central actor, and these persons, while in contact and interaction with each other, do not fit into the definition of a group.[51] All that such a distinction permits us to do is to play at a kind of literary game, examining a number of novels to determine whether we shall call them collective or complex.

Prejudices have been created against the "individualistic" novel, and for the "collective" novel. Some seem to feel that an "individualistic" novel has petty bourgeois survivals, whereas the collective novel is free of such taints. And, in addition, the collective novel permits the novelist, in terms

[50] *New Masses*, April 10, 1934.
[51] *Ibid.*

of these prejudices, to convey a clearer sense of groups and classes. Often such a prejudice amounts to the following assumption: you cannot convey so complete a sense of a class or a group if you treat one member of it in extensive detail and in interaction with others as you can if you treat many members of a class in relatively the same space, but pay much less detailed attention to any individual. Such a theory almost falls over backward into mysticism.

John Dos Passos' *The 42nd Parallel* has been praised as a collective novel; though I find no important difference between the way in which he seeks to establish character and the way in which many "individualistic" novelists seek to establish theirs. The characters in *The 42nd Parallel* have thoughts and feelings. They say things. They participate in various actions. They make, or they fail to make, relevant analyses of the meanings of what they say, do, think, and see. This being the case, why transfer a structural difference into another category? The notion that the extent of the geographical territory covered in a novel and a prolixity of characters treated with relatively little detail will convey a stronger sense of the pressure of social circumstances, and a stronger feeling of group or class or continent—this notion is inherently unsound. And it is suggested in Dos Passos, because he has to rely for unity on mechanical interlardings—his news-reel, his camera's eye, his use of free-verse biographies of contemporary and historical figures. Some of these latter sketches, true, are among the finest pieces that he has written. "The Body of An American," in *1919,* for example, is both powerful and moving. I do not criticize it, *per se;* I only suggest here that it seems like something mechanically added to his book in order to attain unity, and that such attempts are technically obvious.

I do not contend that collective novels cannot be written. Two of the finest war novels that I have ever read are to be classified as collective novels— Theodor Plivier's *The Kaiser's Coolies* and *The Kaiser Goes, The Generals Remain.* I do think, however, that many collective novels written in America are dissipated in their total impact. The use of many characters forces the author to be most accurate and careful in his use of details to establish a sense of people and of life. And our collective novelists have, I think, in most cases failed to achieve this. Also I think that this type of novel is frequently written because novelists cannot sustain the development of an individual character and hold the reader's interest over a span of three, four, or five hundred pages; just as many play-wrights, consciously or unconsciously aware of their inability to sustain a few characters through three acts, and to establish convincing relationships between them, fill their up stage with characters, and trust to luck and the tolerance of the audience.

If my analysis and argument be sound, it follows that any hierarchy of values in novels according to their form—whether, that is, they are collective, complex, or individualistic—is meaningless. Distinctions must be of another order. It is apparent that human beings, no matter what group or social class they belong to, do not always function *consciously* as members of group or class. Sometimes, to themselves they seem to function alone. While they exist in situations of interaction with other human beings, and with human beings in groups and classes, and while groups and classes, and more generally, society, always possess a potential or an actual conditioning and controlling effect upon their conduct, it still remains that their conduct cannot be completely understood if it is apprehended merely in terms of the simplified reflex from a group or class stimulus. Besides being members of classes and groups, they are intractable individual entities, each uniquely different in some respects from every other human being on this planet. Their sensations, their thoughts, their experiences are not complete copies of the sensations, thoughts, and experiences of any other human being. Thus, if one takes a large enough number of people about whom a sufficient number of data are known, it is possible to predict statistically how the component parts of such a number will react to a given and fairly familiar situation or stimulus. It can be predicted with a fair degree of accuracy how many of this number will (say) react in one pattern, and how many in another. It cannot, however, be predicted how any single individual of that number will react. In other words, in every individual there is an aspect of uniqueness and intractability, and this makes him not completely predictable in every potential situation.

A novelist in developing his characters is concerned not only with the fact that they belong to a group or a class, and that that group or class is a conditioning factor in their conduct; he is not concerned only with the fact that his characters have many resemblances to other human beings, and are subject, along with the rest, to the working and the necessities of a whole series of natural laws, including the laws that define the working of social processes. He is concerned, as well, with his characters as unique and distinct from other human beings with whom they have common experiences, and to whom they show certain human resemblances.

Proust, in *Within a Budding Grove* (Random House), has a most excitingly exact description of certain impressions of a railroad journey taken by the "I" of the novels; followed by some illuminating remarks that can be shown to bear on my analysis here:

"We invariably forget that these [qualities in the sights he saw, the sunrise, etc.] are individual qualities, and, substituting for them in our mind a conventional type at which we arrive by striking a sort of mean amongst the different faces that have taken our fancy, the pleasures we have known, we are left with mere abstract images which are lifeless and dull because they are lacking in precisely that element of novelty, different from anything we have known, that element which is proper to beauty and to happiness. And we deliver on life a pessimistic judgment which we suppose to be fair, for we believed that we were taking into account when we formed it happiness and beauty, whereas in fact we left them out and replaced them by syntheses in which there is not a single atom of either. So it is that a well-read man will at once begin to yawn with boredom when anyone speaks to him of a new 'good book', because he imagines a sort of composite of all the good books that he has read and knows already, whereas a good book is something special, something incalculable, and is made up not of the sum of all previous masterpieces but of something which the most thorough assimilation of every one of them would not enable him to discover, since it exists not in their sum but beyond it."

So it is with a character in a novel, no matter what class he belongs to. He is not just a copy of all the other members of his class.[52] He is a person with resemblances to all the other members of that class, and with a difference from all the other members of that class. The novelist is concerned not merely with either the similarities or the differences, but with both of them; this statement bears emphasis and repetition. General theses, classroom instruction about forms, about the superior

[52] "History makes itself in such a way that the final result always arises from conflicts between many individual wills, of which each again has been made what it is by a host of particular conditions of life. Thus there are innumerable intersecting forces, an infinite series of parallelograms of forces which give rise to one resultant—the historical event. This again may itself be viewed as the product of a power which, taken as a whole, works *unconsciously* and without volition. For what each individual wills is obstructed by everyone else, and what emerges is something that no one willed. Thus past history proceeds in the manner of a natural process and is also essentially subject to the same laws of movement. But from the fact that individual wills—of which each desires what he is impelled to by his physical constitution and external, in the last resort, economic circumstances (either his own personal circumstances or those of society in general) do not attain what they want, but are merged into a collective mean, a common resultant, it must not be concluded that their value $= 0$. On the contrary each contributes to the resultant and is to this degree involved in it." *Marx-Engels, Selected Correspondence*, No. 213, pp. 476–7.

value of one type of novel over another, are meaningless, particularly in respect to the effort of the novelist to convey this sense of the uniqueness of his characters. The collective novel is not, by any *a priori* theory or assumption, going to enable the novelist to write a better novel.

Such theses on the collective novel are generally tied up with Marxian concepts such as the class struggle. Applied in the wholesale they add a formalized viewpoint to the formalization of a structure for the novelist; they tend to present the collective novel as a direct outgrowth of Marxian concepts, and even to imply that the collective novel is the means of embodying, in creative literature, a Marxian interpretation and Marxian concepts. This means—in the words of Joseph Freeman [53]—proceeding from "the general to the specific instead of from the specific to the general." I think Freeman is correct in suggesting that the creative process is the latter, except that a qualification is demanded: the statement should be broadened to indicate that the specific and the general are not to be juxtaposed. The writer's procedure is from both the specific and the general; that is to say, he utilizes specific impressions and predicaments, and also general ideas. Without gen-

[53] Introduction to *Proletarian Literature in the United States.*

eral ideas it is impossible to understand specific meanings, and the specific remains unconnectedly specific. The writer never leaves the specific in this state, because this is impossible. Whether a novelist has a consistent body of general ideas or not, he has general ideas, and he uses these in the organization of his material,[54] so that his approach is neither one nor the other, but a relating of both, in both directions. But again, it would be idle, for instance, to invent a new notion, and contend that the "collective" novel proceeds from the general, and the "individualistic" novel from the specific; or—to state the same notion in different terms— that the collective novel deals with the general, and the "individualistic" novel with the specific. All these unsound uses of the "general" in applica-

[54] Proust is an example of a novelist equipped with a good stock of general ideas which he utilized in the writing of his works. A student of Bergson, he brought into the novel philosophical conceptions of time and change; and this equipment enabled him to introduce, with much effect, the phenomenon of "psychological relativity" into literature, applied concretely and specifically.

Dreiser, on the contrary, is an example of a novelist—and, in my opinion, a great novelist—equipped with a bad stock of general ideas. His materialism tends to be mechanical, and he posits it as a kind of lump opposed to man; to this mechanical materialism there is added a mystical conception of the non-existence of the individual. Thus, formally, he is unable to attain a sufficiently clear-cut sense of the world as process, of the fact of the individual human being, as an individual human being, in interaction with other human beings in society, and in interaction with nature through society. It remains, though, that he does have general ideas, even though they be not clear-cut.

121

tion constitute what Whitehead has aptly termed "the fallacy of misplaced concretion"—the assumption that abstract ideas are not a reference or a copy or an abstraction from specific realities, but are existent, specific realities, not only in their proper situation (which is the human consciousness) but also in the external world.

Another sentence from Proust's *Within a Budding Grove* will bear quotation: "As a rule it is with our being reduced to a minimum that we live, most of our faculties lie dormant because they can rely upon Habit, which knows what there is to be done and has no need of their services." Sights on the railroad journey were the stimulating means which called upon the "I" of the novels to utilize such faculties, presenting "a project which would have the further advantage of providing with subject matter the selfish, active, practical, mechanical, indolent, centrifugal tendency which is that of the human mind." Often we rely on habit and a generalized memory when we use generalized statements, formulations, and the like as a substitute for the reception of fresh and new impressions from concrete reality. We do not analyze our new impressions; we do not explore our past in order to attain a greater and more vividly rich sense of characters, sights, and events, but rather we allow

122

them to slip into generalized memories. Then we use our "ideas" as a cover for these indolent habits and practices.

In reading and criticizing literature, we can allow the same slothfulness of habit to become a substitute for the understanding of literature and the exercise of judgment. We can, for instance, formulate definitions of the types of the novel that should be written. Out of these definitions we can create formal distinctions, formal categories, and then use these as the groundwork for the erection of hierarchies. When we hierarchize different types of the novel, in terms of content alone or structure alone, this is the precise result that we achieve.

§ 3

Extra-literary distinctions, as well as the confused use of the categories *bourgeois* and *proletarian* in critical writing, have been the product of a crass and oversimplified utilization of the Marxian concept of the class struggle. This concept, as I understand it, posits that social classes exist objectively in society. These classes are determined by economic and material relationships. A man's membership in any class is determined by his economic status, and by the relationships in which this status places him with other men. Out of these relationships there develops a contradiction, a conflict of interests, and this contradiction or conflict begets class struggle. The basis of the class struggle in a capitalist society lies in the fact that one class controls the means of production, and uses this control in order to exploit the class which requires the use of the means of production in order to create goods for society and in order to earn its livelihood.

It further posits that the history of societies, and the changes in societies from one form to another, are the result of class struggle. Inasmuch as material relationships determine thought originally, it follows that the problems men face, the situations in which they find themselves, the societies in which they live, are controlling factors in what they say, do, feel, think, and even want. It follows that the class struggle, which cuts down to the core of social relations, and the class to which a man belongs, are *essential* causal factors in determining that man's ideals, feelings, and habit mechanisms. This means that we can say, objectively, that a man belongs to a social class, and the fact that he belongs to a social class affects other spheres and features in his life besides the purely economic ones.

INDIVIDUALISM AND THE CLASS STRUGGLE

But how does the class struggle make its impact upon the life of the individual? It comes into his consciousness by dictating his relations to other men: It delimits the kind of life that he may or may not live. It builds up habits of response and thinking, of which he may or may not be aware. It sets within him many potentialities of action which will be realized and expressed internally or overtly in terms of the objective situations. The class struggle, however, does not in any sense produce so complete a differentiation of human beings that there are no similarities between men who, objectively, belong to different social classes. Nor does it mean that the class struggle is a direct, potent, conscious factor at every moment in a man's life; it does not cause him to act in every detail of every situation in a preconditioned way that makes him indistinguishable from other members of his class. The class struggle is not something that the worker breathes, so that he goes about breathing two parts of ozone to one part of class struggle. It is an objective set of relationships, fundamental in a society, and it has a devious, shifting, differentiating influence (sometimes direct, sometimes indirect) on individuals and on classes. We cannot, then, treat the class struggle as if it were just some lumpy force pushing men in an equal and co-ordinate way toward two sides of a barricade where they will proceed to fire guns and throw bricks at each other. I repeat, therefore, that the class struggle, as I understand it, is a fundamental set of relationships, and that out of this fundamental set there grow many potentialities of conduct, of thought, feeling, dream, fantasy, as well as of overt action. And I say that the class struggle is not, for the Marxist, simply an article of faith. It is something that he examines, traces, correlates, understands.

One of the fundamental mistakes in various "leftist" tendencies has been the treatment of the class struggle either as a fixed absolute or else as an article of sentimental faith. In either case, hypostatization has taken place, the result of which has been that "leftists" in attempting to analyze various types of economic and cultural phenomena have lacked the equipment and the flexibility to apprehend and intellectually organize their understanding of society as a process. This explains why they have lost sight of the fact that to a Marxist there is cultural unity in the sense that a single given and fundamental objective situation and set-up of conditions will produce an infinite diversity of cultural manifestations. The first duty of a Marxist critic is neither to condemn these cultural manifestations *per se*, nor to lump them into categories of

bourgeois and *proletarian,* and there let them lie.
His first duty is to understand them, to understand
where and how they interconnect with other manifestations, and from this interconnection to grasp
their meanings.

Granville Hicks has been described by John
Strachey in *Literature and Dialectical Materialism*
(Covici-Friede) as "the foremost Marxist literary
critic of America." Hicks has defended Marxist
criticism in America today in these words [55]:

"A genuinely comprehensive system was at the moment impossible. At least we freed revolutionary criticism from an untenable dualism, and more than that,
we also, I believe, indicated certain important general
principles that any comprehensive system must take into
account."

I suspect that Mr. Hicks allowed his enthusiasm
to carry him away when he wrote this. For when
one glances back over the products of much of our
"Marxist" criticism, where does one find that freedom from the old dualism of the *Masses* critics
like Floyd Dell? Is an excess of functional extremism the means of freeing literature from dualism?
Is the mechanical forging of "important general
principles" the means of laying the foundation for

[55] In *The American Writers' Congress.*

127

establishing a comprehensive system? Is the mechanical application of the concept of the class struggle a step forward, or a detour into irrelevancy? To consider a specific example from *The Great Tradition*, we may ask what principle Mr. Hicks was forging when he wrote "From *Walden* the men of the post-war generation could learn how to live if they wished to abandon forever the fruit of industrial progress, but they were by no means willing to make such a renunciation, nor could they have made it had they so desired. What they needed was someone to humanize their faith in the machine and make it discriminating, and with that problem Thoreau had no concern."

Here it is appropriate to quote the remarks of William Phillips and Philip Rahv, editors of the *Partisan Review and Anvil*.[56] " 'Leftism' is not an accidental practice, nor can it be regarded merely as youthful impetuosity. Its literary 'line' stems from the understanding of Marxism as mechanical materialism. In philosophy, mechanical materialism assumes a direct determinism of the whole superstructure by the economic foundation, ignoring the dialectical interaction between consciousness and environment, and the reciprocal influence of the parts of the superstructure on each

[56] *Proletarian Literature in the United States*, p. 370.

other and on the economic determinants. The literary counterpart of mechanical materialism faithfully reflects this vulgarization of Marxism. But its effects strike even deeper: it paralyzes the writer's capacities by creating a dualism between his artistic consciousness and his beliefs, thus making it impossible for him to achieve anything beyond fragmentary, marginal expression." [57]

The mechanistic methods of "leftism" have been damaging in two important ways. First, writers

[57] "When Communists, in *New Masses* and *International Literature*, criticize proletarian literature, they are always safe when they can attack the writer ideologically. If the writer is ideologically sound, they express naïve surprise that his book is not readable, coupled with heartfelt hopes that the proletariat will soon do better. They have no criterion or critical apparatus by which to offer the most elementary explanations of mere inefficiency. I imagine that to the perfect Communist literary critic it must be a matter of almost dumbfounded astonishment that a Chinese coolie who is a member of the party cannot write books far better than the bourgeois propaganda of Shakespeare." *The Destructive Element*, by Stephen Spender, pp. 254-5. Houghton Mifflin Co.

For "Communist" here, the word "leftist" should be substituted. Mr. Spender is speaking precisely of leftism which in this volume is described as a functional extremism. I quote his remark to show the results of leftism. It is an influence that alienates even those sympathetic to the revolutionary movement. It is because of leftism that "ideological" criticism runs to all its extreme of rampant irrelevancy. Examples of such leftism have been overplenty in both the *New Masses* and *International Literature*, and the degree of their danger cannot be more illustratively indicated than by the very nature and tone of Mr. Spender's remark, and by the fact that it has been given so much justification by leftists. This being the situation, it is far, far too early to talk of what we have accomplished by way of unification and forging of fundamental principles. If fundamental principles produce such results, and from such sympathetic sources, it is more than clear that they had better be entirely reforged.

have been led to create characters out of concepts
—"the general"—instead of from life with the
clarifying assistance that concepts provide. The result of this has been obviousness. The characters
often illustrate concepts that have not been
soundly applied. Second, such work has been un-
duly encouraged and praised, so that it has been
tacitly set up as a literary model to be followed. In
order to establish such unrewarding writing as a
model, critics and reviewers have gone a step
farther. They have utilized such models and the
concepts they present, in order to diminish the
reputation and the understanding of novels that
do not conform to the standards governing this
type. The novels thus regarded as models have generally restated ideas that have been repeatedly
developed in books, articles, pamphlets, and editori-
als. [58] In other words, they are a rehash, contributing no new understanding, giving no concrete
sense of life and no help in the application of the
concepts. Abstractions have merely been allowed
to walk in at the wrong place.

[58] A parallel here is to be found in the utilization often made of Freud
in an earlier period. There we found writers turning life into a repetition
of a Freudian concept of the libido. On one hand, this was repetition
of what was already available in psycho-analytic literature; it contributed
nothing new. Hence, it had nothing to say. On the other hand, it became the means of over-simplification.

It was against all such tendencies and practices that Waldo Frank inveighed at the American Writers' Congress: [59] "Briefly, I will disclose symptoms and attitudes in our revolutionary writers, which reveal (although the writers know it not)" a "sterile philosophy." He listed symptoms of this, among them:

"Disbelief in the autonomy of the writer's art; in its integral place *as art* in the organic growth of man and specifically in the revolutionary movement. This self-distrust makes the writer capitulate *as artist*: leads him to take orders, *as artist,* from political leaders—much to the dismay of the more intelligent of said political leaders . . . the servile or passive concept of revolutionary literature as primarily 'informational', 'reflective' 'propaganda' . . . borrowed from the mid-Victorian, middle-class idea of utilitarian or moralistic art. . . . What murder is to the art of life, this dead philosophy is to knowledge; and translated into literary terms, it becomes 'over-simplification'. Call it, if you prefer, a kind of misplaced or *forced* direct-action. Here are some of its results: . . . Novels aiming to reveal . . . revolutionary portent . . . stuffed with stereotypes . . . Proletarian tales and poems which portray the workers as half-dead people devoid of the imagination . . . Laborious essays in criticism and literary history in which the organic bodies of the works of poets and

[59] "Values of the Revolutionary Writer," the *American Writers' Congress.*

131

prose-men are mangled and flattened to become mere wall-papering for the structure of a political argument." [60]

[60] Waldo Frank and I here arrive at essentially the same conclusions, though not, I think, from the same premises. His starting point is— or so I assume, from what I have read of his work—a concept of the whole man, described as "a sense of the whole" in his *The Rediscovery of America*.

So far as I was able to interpret that book, it had two points. One, it argued for a sense of the whole man as the basis for the rediscovery of America. Two, it posited a sense of cultural unity which must be put to drastic revision if it is to be co-ordinated into a Marxist viewpoint. This conception of cultural unity belongs to that of the national liberal school of American criticism. It suggests that America is composed, as it were, of the dead fragments of a former cultural unity— that is, the medieval ages. The transplanting of these dead fragments into America has resulted in the failure to attain an American culture that is an organic whole. The result is a borrowed and a fragmentary culture. From that, it is deducible that the American man is fragmentary. If he attains this sense of the whole, he leads the way toward the larger cultural and organic unification of American life and American culture. A similar but less mystical view is to be found in Lewis Mumford's *The Golden Day;* and its conclusion is a call to lead the way to a new golden day.

These ideas, calling for organic development, seem to me to be unorganic, inasmuch as they assume a cultural unity on the basis of a society that is fundamentally a disunity in the sense that it is developed on the base of contrasting and conflicting social classes. Cultural unity in the Marxist sense, I assume, means that a given economic and material set-up is the fundamental source of diverse manifestations.

A second error in the thought of this school is the lack of a sense of change and of the meaning of change. The medieval society was not only a unity, in their sense; it was also a society in which there were social classes. It broke up as the result of a class conflict. That break-up resulted in a new society—the bourgeois democratic state, which in turn assimilated some of the former cultural elements, and added onto that its own cultural developments. It is this omission, as well as, in Mumford's case (*Technics and Civilization*), explicit confusions as to the nature of Marxism, that negates this analysis. Failing to take into consideration the basis of society in social classes, this school gives man a false place in the development and changing of society.

Waldo Frank has gravitated from this position to one that affirms the revolutionary movement. In a paper of his, "The Writer's Part in Communism" (*Partisan Review and Anvil*, February, 1936), we can see suggestions of his shifting emphasis, of his change of viewpoint since the writing of *The Rediscovery of America*. However, in his use of the word *organic* I still see mysticism. In this paper he speaks of "the validity and primacy of man's intuitive organic sense." This appeal to intuition is the basis for creating the harmony of the whole man who can function properly within "the social body." I cannot accept his sense (as I understand it) of the word "organic"; though I do not admit that the dissociation of myself from this feature of his view invalidates the comments that I have quoted from him. Nor does it destroy the validity of certain emphases he makes in his writings— his objection to the conception of man as merely the passive product of environment, and his emphasis on the validity of cultural values and their interpretation, not merely as the mute products of economics but also as the product of previous cultural manifestations.

CHAPTER X

Literature and Propaganda

CLOSELY connected with a mechanistic utilization of the concept of class struggle, there has
arisen a confusing use of the slogan "All art is
propaganda." Already, in America, a great deal
of energy has been wasted in bad expositions and
feeble defenses of this formula.

Lenin's ideas on propaganda in *What Is To Be
Done?* (International Publishers) are worth presenting here, though we must understand that his
discussion is not directly concerned with creative
literature in the form of the novel; rather it treats
of the dissemination of theoretical information and
of political ideas.

"We thought . . . that a propagandist dealing with
say the question of unemployment must explain the
capitalistic nature of crises, the reasons why crises are
inevitable in modern society, must describe how present
society must inevitably become transformed into Social-

ist society, etc. In a word, he must present 'many ideas', so many indeed that they will be understood as a whole only by a (comparatively) few persons. An agitator, however, speaking on the same subject will take as an illustration a fact that is most widely known and outstanding among his audience—say the death from starvation of the family of an unemployed worker, the growing impoverishment, etc.—and utilising this illustration, will direct all his efforts to present *a single idea* to the 'masses', i.e., the idea of the senseless contradiction between the increase of wealth and increase of poverty. . . . Consequently, the propagandist operates chiefly by means of the *printed* word; the agitator operates with the *living* word. The qualities that are required of an agitator are not the same as the qualities that are required of a propagandist. Kautsky and Lafargue, for example, we call propagandists; Bebel and Guesde we call agitators. . . . Take, for example, the struggle now being carried on by the German Social-Democrats against the grain duties. The theoreticians write researches in tariff policy and 'call', say, for a fight for commercial treaties and for free trade. The propagandist does the same thing in the periodical press, and the agitator does it in public speeches."

Joseph Freeman,[61] in discussing literature, frankly declares that "art, an instrument in the class struggle, must be developed by the prole-

[61] *Proletarian Literature in the United States*, p. 9 et seq.

tariat as one of its weapons." He associates art
with politics, but also says that "to characterize
an essay or a book as a political pamphlet is neither
to praise nor to condemn it." He distinguishes art
as something different from action and from science, and as "distinct from party program." Art
is, he says, the communication of experience. However—

"the catch lies in the word 'experience.' The liberal
critic . . . wants us to believe that when you write
about the autumn wind blowing a girl's hair or about
'thirsting breasts', you are writing about 'experience';
but when you write about the October Revolution, or
the Five-Year-Plan, or the lynching of Negroes in the
South, or the San Francisco Strike, you are not writing
about 'experience'. Hence to say 'bed your desire among
the pressing grasses' is *art;* while *Roar China,* Mayakov-
sky's poems, or the novels of Josephine Herbst and
Robert Cantwell are *propaganda.*"

Freeman is here guilty of simplification. His
statements about "the liberal critic" are not completely true. For instance, one of his curious
omissions is the fact that various liberal critics
and reviewers revealed more understanding of the
work of two writers whom he hails as propagandists—Robert Cantwell and Josephine Herbst—

than did Granville Hicks (say), who purports to be a "Marxian" critic.

To continue, as Freeman says, the question is, "What constitutes experience?" He contends quite rightly that the life of the working classes and the phenomena of the class struggle are part of experience, and that if art is to be severed from the utilization of these, from the "development of knowledge," and from the "technique of scientific action," the only experiences left are "the experience of personal sensation, emotion, and conduct, the experience of the parasitic classes. Such art is produced today by bourgeois writers. Their experience is class-conditioned, but, as has always been the case with the bourgeoisie, they pretend that their values are the values of humanity." Freeman grants what I have called the persistence-value. After granting this value in the art of the past, he says that a more important question is: why does not a writer or a composer today write or compose like the great literary and musical geniuses of the past? The answer is obvious: Social conditions have changed and art is socially conditioned.

Freeman describes then the way in which American writers began to see that art is socially conditioned, and from this, the rapid growth, and the rapid addition of names to the side of revolutionary literature. Speaking of the shift of writers and intellectuals to the left, he declares: "There came a time when many writers who had all their lives ignored politics and economics suddenly abandoned the poem, the novel, and the play and began to write solemn articles on unemployment, fiscal policy, and foreign trade. This politicalization of the man of letters was a step toward his transformation *as a poet*." Such a remark leaves me dubious. I see no grounds for objection when the poet, the novelist, or the playwright abandons his craft to write articles on fiscal policy and foreign trade; though it may be a dubious enterprise if he does not assimilate the material relevant to the subjects he treats. And it seems to me that the politicalization of our men of letters leaves many of them still in a state of confusion, and makes for much shallow writing.

Freeman does not mention the directions in "Marxist" literary thought which I have been discussing; indeed, he lays a coat of whitewash over them. It is only natural, then, that one should be reminded of a remark from Lenin's *What Is To Be Done?* "But can anything more 'shallow' be imagined than an opinion of a whole tendency that is based on nothing more than what the representatives of that tendency say about themselves?"

He does not, however, clear up the question of propaganda for us, though, except for his coat of whitewash on "leftist" tendencies, and his failure to represent properly the attitudes and viewpoints of liberal critical thought, he talks sense—and I hold that it is always a virtue to talk sense. Thus, to repeat one of his remarks: "Art at its best does not deal with abstract anger. When it does it becomes abstract and didactic. The best art deals with specific experience which arouses specific emotion in specific people at a specific moment in a specific locale, in such a way that other people who have had similar experiences in other places and times recognize it as their own." This comment, however, demands qualifying elaboration. It must not be construed as implying that the best art is one of pure immediacy, thus sanctioning pure immediacy in art. Also, it should be added that art gives people a sense of recognition of experience, and an understanding of other experience that they may not always recognize as their own. Art, besides allowing recognition of the familiar, sometimes creates also the ability to assimilate and recognize the unfamiliar. If it did not or could not achieve such a result, it could not be the means for the expansion of experience. Therefore, if Freeman's characterization of art be taken as it stands, it leads to the conclusion that art is completely circumscribed by class—whereupon we shall fall back into our trap of mechanical applications of the concept of the class struggle. His definition will then be a re-enforcement of dogma and sectarianism, blinding us in our consideration of propaganda. He asserts an affirmation of propaganda, but fails to elucidate further.

§ 2

Reverting to Lenin's remarks on propaganda, we note that he specified certain functions in the dissemination of political ideas—those of the propagandist and the agitator. Moreover, we see—in the practices of the German Social-Democratic party of his time—the way in which an issue was fought with a definite practising of separate, if connected, functions on the part of the theoreticians, the propagandists, and the agitators. We cannot completely transfer to literature Lenin's delegation of the function of the political propagandist in politics, because literature is not completely concerned with the presentation of a body of ideas, as ideas, systematized and connected; it is not satisfactorily adapted to perform such a task. Rather it is chiefly concerned with life in the raw, with end results and end manifestations, not usually with genetic bases such as the ultimate economic point of origin of a cultural or "social" manifestation. If the novelist aims to present a system of ideas as ideas, the result will be that he will end not as a novelist but as a theoretician. And while there is no inherent objection to the novelist turning theoretician, if he has the necessary mental equipment, it remains that when he does so he is delegating to himself another function —the theoretician's—which we are not discussing here. Our direct interest is rather the function of the literary artist *qua* artist.

Literature, as part of the social superstructure, by its very nature, lags behind the swift movement of events and imaginatively anticipates them. In any case, it need not, and does not, march military fashion in step with their actual development.

To quote Maxim Gorky from *On Guard for the Soviet Union* (International Publishers) : "Nobody can seriously bewail the fact that literature is lagging behind reality. It has always followed in the wake of life, it has always 'recorded facts', generalized about them, given them synthesis. No one ever demanded of a writer that he be a prophet and foretell the future!"

From these remarks it should be clear that we

cannot transfer Lenin's statement about propaganda, applying it point by point, without change, to the sphere of literature, since the latter performs a function different from that of political theory and political propaganda.

This point is illuminated if we contrast two definite works. *The Communist Manifesto* is political propaganda, and it is also now recognized by many as a literary masterpiece. Does the fact that it is a literary masterpiece alter its content? If it were not a literary masterpiece, if its style were wooden or difficult, would this feature destroy the soundness, the validity, the applicability of its ideas? Malraux's *Man's Fate,* even if not a literary masterpiece, is considered by many to be one of the finest works of contemporary letters. This also is political in its content. Its narrative presents political ideas, an interpretation of an historic political event, the Chinese revolution. Its political features have provoked controversy. Does the soundness or the unsoundness of its political interpretation destroy its validity as a work of literature? At least some of the critics and commentators who have challenged it on political grounds have granted it recognition on literary grounds. For whether its political interpretation and its direct political implications be *politically* sound or unsound, it retains its powerful emotional drive; it conveys a sense of the Chinese revolution and of characters participating in it; achieving this, it intensifies our awareness. Hence we can see that *The Communist Manifesto* would be sound political propaganda whether or not its style made it a literary masterpiece; and *Man's Fate* remains a moving and powerful work of literature, regardless of the soundness or unsoundness of its politics. In other words, political propaganda and creative literature are not *precisely* the same.

In America the word *propaganda* has sometimes been used almost in the sense in which Lenin used *agitation,* except that this latter function was to be performed only by the spoken word. In addition, the word *propaganda* in America has, thanks to the World War and commercial advertising, been given a different meaning from the one given to it in the translations of Lenin's works. I am therefore going to offer, as a basis for this discussion, a definition of the word.

I shall here define propaganda as the scheme or plan or process or technique of propagating a system, a scheme, an idea or set of ideas, a doctrine, or an attitude or attitudes, all with the aim of producing a proposed course of action, or else of producing acquiescence in a proposed course of action.

I think that my definition applies to many of the references to propaganda to be found in the reviews and articles of our American revolutionary critics who have discussed the subject. For their emphasis is on action, on not only interpreting the world but also changing the world. When one tries to persuade or convince large masses of people—to propagate ideas among them—one will hardly succeed if one ignores the appropriate methods, or is unaware of certain important facts. One must know how large masses of people are unified, how their attention may be directed toward certain goals, and toward the actions that will enable them to achieve these goals. In propagating an attitude, idea, doctrine, system of ideas, or course of action in the minds of large masses, it is necessary to find common denominators and to eliminate disturbing and contradictory suggestions; otherwise an insufficient unity of will and action will be attained.

One of the instruments of propaganda, in the sense in which I have here defined it, is the slogan. The application of propaganda to the solution of social problems is absolutely essential. Propaganda has its definite place, its methods, its values, its necessities. It is, for instance, characteristic of a great leader that the slogans he formulates present a progressive answer to the needs of an objective situation; also that they are part of the program of a long-run policy that is progressive in the Marxian sense; and finally that his slogans contain the potentialities for elaborating policies and methods that will serve as an outline for answering the needs of the objective situation to which they are referred, and of solving, in a progressive Marxian sense, the problems which these needs bring forth.

An illustration here is the slogans which Lenin forged during the days preceding the October Revolution in 1917. He stenciled, in effective slogans, the answer to the problems in Russia at that time and the needs of the Russian masses. These slogans established the basis for achieving the fundamental unity of action necessary in proceeding toward the solution of these problems. Implicit within them were the potentialities for the establishment of the Soviet Government in Russia.

One difference beween Lenin's propaganda—his slogans for peace, land, and bread, for the achievement of these ends through the giving of power to the Soviets, etc.—and the propaganda and slogans of a demagogue is apparent. The latter consist in statements or promises that cannot be fulfilled—they are slogans that do not logically contain the necessary potentialities for progressive action in the Marxian sense. A second difference is that Lenin's slogans were a concise description of the ends and the basis of action, carrying policies into effect; whereas the demagogue's slogans are usually the means by which the implementing of effective, progressive policies is prevented. In short, Lenin meant his slogans, and the demagogue does not mean his. Moreover, Lenin's slogans did not degrade thought; on the contrary, they were a precise expression of policies, and thus were the exact opposite of the demagogue's.

Lenin's slogans were effective propaganda in the best sense of the term. However, are we going to interpret the slogan "All art is propaganda" to mean the forging of slogans dealing with political policies? To such a critic as Joseph Freeman, this is not the intended meaning. In others, however, there is a confusion of meanings, and with this, an evident misconception of functions. To quote a statement by Jack Conroy: [62] "To me a strike bulletin or an impassioned leaflet are of more moment than three hundred prettily and faultlessly written pages about the private woes of a gigolo or the biological ferment of a society dame as useful to society as the buck brush that infests Missouri cow pastures and takes all the sustenance

[62] *The American Writers' Congress*, p. 83.

out of the soil." Though I need hardly say that I favor proper strike bulletins and effective and impassioned leaflets, I see no necessity for counterposing these to works of literature. I agree with Mr. Conroy that the private woes of a gigolo are not particularly interesting, and yet, offhand, it occurs to me that Colette's *Chéri* does describe these private woes with such insight that I was genuinely interested in them; though my liking for *Chéri* certainly would not prevent me from reading a strike bulletin, or an impassioned leaflet, or Lenin's *'Left-Wing' Communism: An Infantile Disorder*. If Mr. Conroy is here referring to Proust—since Proust did write about society dames who were not noted for their usefulness to society—why, my answer is only the more emphatically the same. I assume that there is a unity in society as I have defined it, that there are many manifestations from a given set of objective conditions, and finally that the more deeply one is aware of these manifestations, emotionally as well as intellectually, the better one will succeed in understanding contemporary society.

There seems to be here a mixing-up of the tactics required for the rôles of agitator, strike leader, political leader, Marxian theoretician, and novelist. One man may be all of these, serve more than one of these valuable functions, but when he does so, he must—if he is to succeed—perform these various functions according to their internal logic and necessities. Politics is obviously concerned with government and with the solution of social problems. It must find answers that are embodied in action. Literature, by contrast, is not so directly concerned with finding answers to social problems that will be immediately embodied in action; and, generally speaking, novelists and poets are not equipped to serve as political leaders. In addition, the process itself of producing literature denies the validity of literature's serving as an effective means of propaganda as I have defined it. Works of literature are, generally, not quickly enough assimilated to become instruments of propaganda leading to the choice of immediate courses of action. The social scene, particularly in unstable times like the present, is too shifting, too changing, to permit literature frequently to act toward the immediate solution of social problems. By the time a writer can assimilate material essential for a novel about a social problem, think through the potentialities of his material, arrange and write it, check his sources, rewrite it, finish it for publication, and correct the proofs—by that time one, two, or three years may have elapsed. After this, more time is needed for the distribution of the novel, and for its assimilation by its readers. And, as likely as not, by that time the social and class relationships will have shifted and altered. For the process of assimilating a novel sometimes takes years. Proust, for instance, is still in the process of being assimilated; so is Joyce. So is Shakespeare, for that matter, as Mr. Morrow's work suggests.

More important, many literary works do not receive a wide enough distribution [63] in our time to give them much effectiveness in any immediate sense as instruments of propaganda. Thus Henry Hart,[64] a novelist with considerable experience in the publishing business, has discussed the sales of certain revolutionary novels that were written with an avowedly propagandist intent. These books received satisfying and—in some cases—even "selling" reviews. Yet in the group the largest sale was 3,000 copies. Another sold 2,700, but of this number 1,000 were disposed of at a considerable discount. The sale of a third had not reached 1,200. In view of these figures it is evident that the ob-

[63] "What the Proletariat Reads" by Louis Adamic, in the *Saturday Review of Literature*, Dec. 1, 1934, revealed that the workers by and large do not read novels that are issued often as propaganda for workers. This being the case, it clearly illustrates that propaganda which does not reach its audience in any measurable degree is, to say the very least, a curious brand of propaganda.

[64] "Contemporary Publishing and the Revolutionary Writer," in *The American Writers' Congress*, p. 159 *et seq*.

jective social situation in America is such that this kind of novel cannot have any immediate large-scale effect. When revolutionary novels sell in such relatively small numbers, it is merely talking through one's hat to assert that they can serve as fiery instruments, changing word into deed overnight, or to tell the novelist of today that he must write the novel that will immediately change the world.

When literature has been urged to meet the requirements of limited conceptions of propaganda, the result has most often been the production of ineptitudes. The field of poetry, for instance, has been glutted with inept efforts during the last three or four years. Sometimes poets seeking to express revolutionary sentiments have apparently assumed that there is some necessary connection between bravery and bold-face type. Again, there has been a pointless use of stereotypes and slogans, whether or not they have had any inherent relation within the poems in which they were used. Any number of poets and versifiers might be cited here to suggest the extent to which revolutionary poetry has been needlessly filled with banality—men such as H. H. Lewis and his like. A contributor to the *New Masses*, John Yost, has aptly described this

150

condition.[65] "If poetry is a weapon, it should do something to the enemy—hit him where he lives. . . . And this it is never going to do as long as it is confined to hymnology. Our poets have got to quit sounding off like the Y. M. C. A. secretaries of the revolution. It is a poor out to say that we should not waste time with all this self-criticism (as incestuous as self-praise), and should just keep on trying . . . to do our best, and then if the workers can't see any use in what we do, they won't bother with it and it will all come out right automatically in the end. That's just the old inevitability-of-the-revolution fatalism in esthetic dress, and pretty shoddy dress at that."

Joseph Freeman and others have found it necessary to insist more than once that Marxism and the revolutionary movement cannot make a poet out of a dub; all that it can do for him is to open up avenues to new experience, and offer clarifying conceptions which will enable him to reinterpret old experience, granted he be an artist. That clarity has not, as yet, been noticeable to a sufficient degree in revolutionary poetry; and this, largely for reasons such as those which John Yost has pointed out. The old fatalism, the old mechanical determinism which has perniciously distorted so much of revolutionary

[65] *On Revolutionary Poetry, New Masses,* Aug. 27, 1935.

critical effort, is to be found in the field of revolutionary poetry. Perhaps the most clear-cut example of such poetry in book form is Robert Gessner's *Upsurge*—an empty, windy exhibition of generalized feeling which turns the work into a graceless editorial chopped up into lines to give it the typographical appearance of a poem.[66] It is the mistaken approval of such work as Gessner's that distorts any sense of values in the judgment of poetry. The specious emphasis on activism—which often remains only a verbal emphasis anyway—usually distorts the proper reading, writing, and criticizing of poetry; it creates a confusion between verbal and actual direct action.

Let me give a concrete example, from an article by Edwin Berry Burgum on the poetry of Spender, Auden, and C. Day Lewis.[67] Mr. Burgum quotes these lines from Stephen Spender:

"through torn-down portions of old fabric let their eyes

[66] As a contrast to *Upsurge*, I should like to refer to Kenneth Fearing's "Dénouement" (in *Poems*, Dynamo Press). It is, in my judgment, a suggestion of what might and can be done in the direction of revolutionary poetry when the poet is not deluding himself that he is an activist and that his poem will manage to run a revolution—in other words, when the poet is talented and sets himself, as a poet, to writing poetry instead of trying to build himself a good revolutionary box score by writing "propaganda" poetry to tell "leftist" sources what they already know.

[67] "Three English Radical Poets," by Edwin Berry Burgum, *Proletarian Literature in the United States*, p. 333–4. Also *New Masses*, July 3, 1934.

Watch the admiring dawn explode like a shell
Around us, dazing us with its light like snow."

Mr. Burgum's comment is: "The passive position of watching the dawn is hardly fitting to the revolutionary; nor should the dawn daze like snow those who under self-discipline have known what to expect and are ready for the next move."

Going on to Auden, Mr. Burgum says that "Auden has not yet made his own union of courage and conviction. Nor ought we expect from an Oxford-bred poet, apparently of a family of Welsh squires, an untroubled acceptance of the radical program." [68] In passing, let me remark that Robert Gessner has described the work of Auden, Spender, and Day Lewis as "transitional poems for transit intellectuals." It is apparent here that the failure to realize differences among categories and functions, the failure to understand that various types of literary activity are to be conducted in terms of their internal logic, leads our critics to irrele-

[68] "In July 1934 an article appeared in *New Masses* attacking Auden, Day Lewis, and myself, because we were aristocrats, athletes, and so on. Auden's parents, it said, were Welsh squires, and we were all of exalted birth. Of course there was no word of truth in these attacks, in fact there was no fact at all in the whole article that was not invented. In any case, the facts, even if true, would to most people have seemed irrelevant. But not to this essayist . . . His humble duty was to discredit us, and that he performed, quite regardless of any sense of truth." Stephen Spender in *The Destructive Element*, p. 234. Houghton Mifflin Co.

vancy after irrelevancy. And their conception of the functions and the uses of propaganda in various kinds of writing becomes a trapdoor for their irrelevancies.

There can be no objection to the writer's dealing with politics in his work, or even to his entering the field of direct political action, *unless* he attempts either of these without assuming the obligations and the responsibilities that they will inevitably impose on him. If he undertakes to write political slogans, for instance, purporting to express the needs and answer the problems that exist objectively in the field of actual politics, the writer owes it to his art, to his own integrity, and to the masses to whom he addresses himself, to understand those problems, and not merely in terms of a generalized solution, but also in their background and details. And there is a further demand on him: that he then utilize his knowledge to forge adequate slogans.[69] Finally, it should be

[69] In *What Is To Be Done?* Lenin remarks, apropos of conditions in Russia over thirty years ago: "Meanwhile, Marxian books were published one after another, Marxian journals and newspapers were published, nearly everyone became a Marxist, Marxism was flattered, the Marxists were courted and the book publishers rejoiced at the extraordinary ready sale of Marxian literature. It is quite reasonable to suppose that among the Marxian novices who were carried away by this stream, there was more than one 'author who got a swelled head. . . .' Quite a number of people, with very little, and even totally lacking in, theoretical training, joined the movement."

demanded of him—indeed his own integrity demands it of him—that he assume the responsibilities not of politics alone but also of literature. Hence, if he is to write poetry or any other so-called creative literature, he must give his political slogans internal relationship with the other features of his work; his writing as a whole must be marked by intrinsic rather than extrinsic conviction. A writer is not revealing political consciousness, he is not helping humanity or the proletariat, when he merely expresses—perhaps in blatant boldface—a few political slogans that he learned yester-

---

It is impossible to think of a person becoming anything describable as a Marxist if he has read Marxist literature only. A Marxist should, I think, if he takes his Marxism seriously, read as much non-Marxist literature as Marxist. He should know what opponents there are to Marxism, how the work of non-Marxists bolsters up Marxism and adds argument to its contentions. Also, and this is more important, a person setting out to apply Marxism must have some theoretical capacity, some ability to absorb ideas, and—instead of using them as labels pasted on other ideas—apply, correlate, and synthesize them. To do this, he cannot be a Marxist if he is familiar with Marxism only.

Thus, if he is going to write about politics in America, he needs to be equipped with more than merely a knowledge of Marxist concepts and principles; he must be equipped with actual and theoretical information concerning American politics. This equipment is often lacking, and the lack produces all sorts of empty talk on politics. And this seems to have been one of the evil results of many intellectuals going "leftward" in a too obvious manner. Apparently, before they became Marxists they had merely a literary background. Suddenly they joined forces with the revolutionary movement. They evidently picked up their ideas at second and third hand, and thus they tackled, not literary impressions, not literary criticism, but ideas from a literary and philosophical background. The result is disastrous to thought all around.

day. Again, it is platitudinous though necessary to repeat that to write about politics one must first assimilate some knowledge of that subject.

Often, as the course of this argument has already suggested, propaganda has been given a shifting meaning. Sometimes it is defined as I have defined it. Again, it is applied to the expression of ideas, attitudes, emotions, or sentiments whether these are positive and affirmative, or negative and non-affirmative. When it is given this meaning, when history is combed to show that this philosopher preached despair, that that poet wrote to make us believe that man is good, and such and such composer wrote symphonies that reveal the lift in the eternal spirit of man, the meaning of the word propaganda is debased, given such shifting connotations that it becomes almost meaningless. And besides its use to suggest the conscious effort of writers to express ideas, we find it used also to express unconscious tendencies. Thus Michael Gold has—as was noted earlier—described W. S. Gilbert as a cultural precursor of Fascism; he also commented on Archibald MacLeish as revealing "the Fascist Unconscious." I am not here trying to prove that literature does not—unwittingly as far as the writer is concerned—reveal motives, tendencies, and the like; for literature does do just that.

My point is that if all these things are propaganda, then the word has an astonishing number of meanings; and if it has, then when we use it to develop an argument we certainly ought to tell our readers which sense we are using it in.

§ 3

Thus far, I have discussed "leftist" interpretations of art as propaganda. Perhaps our analysis will be fuller if we examine the question from another angle. For this there is suggestive material in the epilogue of Malcolm Cowley's *Exile's Return, A Narrative of Ideas* (Norton).

Asking whether the artist ought to devote himself to art or to propaganda, Mr. Cowley replies that such a distinction "conceals a type of metaphysical thinking" which derives from Kantian Idealism. This type of thought presents "a whole series of things supposed to be in eternal opposition—form against matter, art against life, artists against philistines, poetry against science, emotion against reason . . . poetry or art against propaganda. In this last opposition all the others are secretly contained. 'Art' is vision, form, repose, truth and beauty, the eternal, everything that is 'good' for the artist. 'Propaganda' is effort, change,

157

science, philistinism, falsity and ugliness, everything that is artistically 'evil'. Once we have accepted these definitions of art and propaganda, the question of choosing between them seems ridiculous."

Mr. Cowley here suggests that he is doing road work to become a dialectician; he has a thesis, and an antithesis, and he synthesizes them by revealing the synthesis as zero. The distinction between art and propaganda, like the distinction between poetry and science, is unsound because it rests upon "an exploded theory of psychology." This "exploded theory" compartmentalizes human faculties such as will, reason, and imagination, and establishes special efforts as functions of such compartmentalized faculties. And "today we know as a simple matter of record that the universe is actually changing in all its parts," including society. Therefore we cannot conceive of literature, or any effort, in dis-relation from other activities.

Such is the chain of reasoning that enables Mr. Cowley to sweep aside a distinction between art and propaganda as irrelevant, and to reach the conclusion that "writers should devote themselves to writing and painters to painting." He then sees only one remaining distinction—the "personal and practical." If the writer expresses himself from the level of unassimilated beliefs, the result is pretty sure to be bad writing—" 'propaganda' "; if he expresses himself from fully assimilated beliefs, the result will be " 'art'." As to the question of beliefs, the writer faces the class struggle; whether he wants to or not, he will be dragged into it. Mr. Cowley hopes that the writer will get on the right side, because if he doesn't he may find himself on the side he doesn't actually favor. Choosing the side of the proletariat, the writer will find release from solitude and isolation; he will be able to find a viewpoint from which he can correlate and arrange near and far events; he will find that "Values exist again."

I devote so much space to Mr. Cowley's thesis here because, even though it is empty of content, it is a satisfactorily representative example of the subjectivist approach to our problem; and it must be remembered that once we have started on a subjectivist course to solve objective problems, we shall end in the same trap, whether we are intelligent or unintelligent. What is most revealing about Mr. Cowley's theory is that he seems completely unable to look at this problem from outside a subjectivist framework. He must immediately relate it to the romantic "religion of art" which seems to have so intrigued his "lost generation." He forgets, for instance, that even when Art is directed far along the trail to solipsism (as it was in the case of the Symbolists) it still has objective effects in society; and our problem here is the objective effects of art in society. Lacking this necessary perception, he dissolves the problem with a *non-sequitur*. It is palpably indefensible, for instance, to say that there is no distinction between poetry and science, that the distinction commonly implied rests on a false theory of psychology deriving from Idealistic philosophy. And from this it is but a step toward the subjectivist contention that art is merely a question of the individual artist's beliefs.

At one time, a romantic and idealist view of activities flourished. Fixed categories were set up which we now know to be non-existent because the world changes; and since there are no fixed categories, there can be no categories at all. Society's activities may be interconnected, but they are not distinct. They therefore have no objective meanings. What matters is the way we look at them. We are concerned with beliefs; with discovering again that values exist (as if values had not always existed in society!). Mr. Cowley's attitude toward these problems suggests a mathematician trying to prove a problem in Euclid by using the multiplication table. He represents a type of the "literary" mind that fails to see a problem, dissolving it in the individual consciousness. After we read him we are left exactly where we were before.

But the problem must be solved, or revolutionary critical theories will reach an impasse. Distinctions here are absolutely essential. My contention cannot be refuted by the blanket assertion that literature and politics are the same, and that literature is therefore political. If that were so, we should have to subdivide types of political activity. There would be one type directly (in both theory and practice) concerned with the problems, the nature, the backgrounds, the functions, and the processes of government, and—behind these—questions of actual control of the state power in an executive sense. And there would be another type of political activity that interests itself in the writing of lyric poetry, the composition of sonnets, the building of dramas, the production of novels. But these two types of activity, whether or not both are political, do not serve the same functions, and do not operate in terms of the same internal logic. If they are divided off as a category, then they must be further divided into sub-categories. And, in either case, they leave us with the problem of distinctions on our hands.

I have gone into this subject in detail in order to show that we must give propaganda one definite meaning and, when we apply the word, confine ourselves strictly to that meaning. And its meaning should, I think, be that it is that method of epitomizing, presenting, and explaining thought and policy which will lead to active political effort. If this meaning be granted, then propaganda is not always synonymous with literature. Even in this strict sense, of course, literature might on occasion serve a propagandistic function; but this use would not confine it to the limits, nor make it solely obedient to the internal logic, of that function.

The nature of our problem should now be manifest: to perceive and understand exactly what the functions of literature are. My position is that literature does not perform an æsthetic function alone, nor an extra-æsthetic function alone; it performs *both*. What, then, are these functions?

Mr. Cowley, in *Exile's Return, a Narrative of Ideas*, confesses that he does not know the answer to this question. At various times, he says, art has served all kinds of functions, and any single theory of art must necessarily be constricting, whatever its character. There are, however, two functions that he would like to see emphasized above all others. He writes:

"I believe that all good works of literary art have the same fundamental thesis. All of them teach us that life is bigger than life—that life as portrayed by the creative imagination is more intense, more varied, more purposeful or lacking in purpose, more tragic or comic, more crowded with meanings and yet more harmoniously organized than is the life we have been leading day by day." [70]

Art, by making life more than life, enables us to reinterpret our experience in the light of the artist's vision, and "the new values we derive from his work . . . make it [life] seem more poetic, dramatic or novelistic, more sharply distinguished

[70] "We can say in general that in plot, types and fullness of characterization poetic works are far inferior to life. There are only two things in which poetic works might be superior to life—in decoration of a story by the addition of effective accessories and in making the characters harmonize more with the events they take part in. . . . Science does not pretend to superiority over nature—and this is not to its shame. Art should not pretend to superiority over life—which would not humiliate it." *Life and Esthetics*, by N. G. Chernishevski, *International Literature*, Number 10, 1935.

We can see here that Mr. Cowley is arguing for an old view that was long ago countered by Chernishevski in Russia. Old views do not walk off the stage when they have been properly countered; they have a habit of returning again and again. Criticism, in its philosophical aspect, must stand guard against these views. Thus, Mr. Cowley, whether or not he is aware of it, is seeking to smuggle such a view back into our midst. This is why we must analyze it at considerable detail to see precisely what it means, and precisely where it leads to.

163

from the world of nature, in other words, more human."

This leads Mr. Cowley to emphasize a second and related special function that the artist should perform today. It is that

"of humanizing nature, in the sense of making it more fit for human beings to live in. The prehistoric world must have seemed alien and terrible to the first tribes that wandered over the face of it. Vast portions of the world are alien to their descendants today. Before a man can feel at home in any surroundings, whether those of seaside or . . . factory, he must first transform the objects about him by connecting them with human emotions . . . transfusing it [the world] with myth. This last phrase . . . describes an essentially simple operation of the mind. It is what a sailor does by calling his vessel 'she' . . . A poet or a painter does the same thing in a richer and more communicable fashion; he gives things *names and values.*" (Italics mine.)

This view, I repeat, demands close scrutiny, for if this be a function of art, we may have to upset the entire analysis that I have been making.

Mr. Cowley and I agree that the basis of art is life. However, when we experience any aspect of life directly, it calls upon all our senses. There is a competition of both external and internal stimuli, bidding for our attention. The passage of events

in life throws up, as it were, innumerable objects
for our attention, many possibilities for our actions. When our attention and interest center on
one out of these many possibilities, we are performing an act of selection that may be conscious or
unconscious. It may be a purely mechanical reflex, but still it is an act of selection on the part
of our organism. Therefore it is impossible for us
to experience all of life. In order to experience one
phase or possibility, we must discard other phases
or possibilities. When we reproduce in art some object or pattern of experience from life, we again
practise the act of selection. We cannot reproduce
a single object, let alone a pattern of experience,
in all its beauty, in all its relationships, actual and
potential, in all its qualities, surfaces, and contours. To do this is an organismal impossibility; because we cannot experience sufficient of life to
do this. In addition, when we experience through
a work of art, we call on fewer of our senses than
when we experience directly. Hence, when we ask
of art that it be more than life, we are asking not
only for the impossible; we are asking for a downright absurdity.

The contention that art must make life more
than life has important implications, however. It
implies, for one thing, that a part can be greater

than the whole; that is—in this case—that consciousness, will, and purpose can create, through
art, something more than meanings. It denies the
fact that between the actual object or pattern of
experience in life, and its reproduction in art, there
is that diminution which Bergson has aptly described. Anyone who is at all familiar with any
of the arts knows the pain and trouble that this
diminution between the actual object or pattern
and the reproduction causes the artist. How, then,
can we fit such a function of the artist within a
materialistic framework? It is impossible. Materialism says that the basis of all life—of all its expressions and manifestations, no matter how remote
they may be from their original causal sources—
is constituted of events occurring within the framework of the material, natural world. Again, I ask,
how can art make life more than it is? Concealed
within this theory there lurks a familiar old spook;
it is called Idealistic Philosophy.

The second function that Mr. Cowley asks the
artist to perform brings that spook out of his
hiding-place; for this demands that nature be made
more familiar, that it be endowed with human attributes.[71] If art fails to make nature human, the

71 Here I am reminded of a passage in Spinoza: "The less men know
of nature the more easily can they coin fictitious ideas, such as trees

world will be an uncomfortable home for man. So Mr. Cowley contends, and so have many others contended in various ways. How is nature made less terrible and less alien? By being used to man's purposes. Civilized man sees nature through society, and only through society. Working as a member of society, he uses nature for his own purposes, and for the purposes of society. He is enabled to achieve this by the application of scientific method, which gives him an understanding of causal relationships and the ability to predict. He is then able either to harness the energies of nature to human purposes, or else to try to get out of the way of nature's terrible workings when he can predict but cannot harness them. But this is the function of science, not of art. Science adapts nature to man's use. Art makes man more human to himself—it does not make nature more human to man. Here lies one of the distinctions between science and art.[72]

---

speaking, men instantly changed into stones, or into fountains, ghosts appearing in mirrors, something issuing from nothing, even gods changed into beasts and men, and infinite other absurdities of the same kind."

[72] I have frequently encountered Mr. Cowley's contention that there is no real difference between science and poetry. One form of it is that the allegories of science and those of poetry are the same. If this be true, then we make no distinction between an image and a concept, a symbol and a concept. And if a concept is a symbol it is a different kind of symbol from an image. When science says that the formula for water is H_2O, it describes actual relations provable by definite tests.

When Mr. Cowley argues that art make nature more human, he is arguing for precisely the same end that Whitehead argues toward in philosophy; he wants to make art do what Whitehead wants to make philosophy do. Whitehead's philosophical system of "organism" leads, I think, directly to the conclusion that philosophy—that is, thought— animates nature. This being the case, a comparison is here pertinent of Mr. Cowley's view in art and of Mr. Whitehead's in philosophy. Whitehead fashions a new language in order to deal with the familiar philosophical problem of the One and the Many. His conception of the world is of a process of events. The element of oneness in the flux or process of events, where there is always change, is the pattern or enduring form of the event. To this pattern or enduring form, he attaches an organic quality—a "principle of concretion". In each event there is a capacity called prehension, the capacity which, in a river, leads it to run

When a poet says that water is "a mirror of delight" or the like, he is not describing actual relations. When we say that twice two are four, we are presenting not an allegory, but a mathematical fact. Whereas, when we say that a tree standing patiently in the wind is like a Stoic philosopher we are not presenting a fact.

This notion is a dangerous contemporary absurdity—dangerous because it breaks down distinctions that are indispensable if thinking is to be clear. And if it be not clear, how can thinking be useful? Ours is an age in which anti-intellectualism has been allowed to run rampant, and anti-intellectualism is a positive danger.

downhill. It is a form of feeling less complicated in other events than in the complex and animate "event" which we know as the human being. We observe the "principle of concretion" in each natural event through its possession of this capacity called prehension. The conclusion is that the universe at large, and all the events in constant passage within it, possess feeling. What is this feeling? What is its source? It is "the ingression of eternal objects" into the passage of events. And what does that mean? It means God. And what is God? God is "the principle of concretion" in each organic event.

Matter is here dissolved into spirit, the objective into the subjective. Thus, clothed in new terminology, we are presented with a familiar, traditional solution to an ancient philosophical problem. The meaning of this system is, then, that the world is endowed with consciousness, and that man possesses the most complicated and developed form of that consciousness. The clear and evident implication within this system is that matter is produced by consciousness. What precise function does such a theory assign to philosophy? It gives philosophy the rôle of animating nature. To animate nature means what? It means to humanize nature. And so we find Whitehead, a man of unquestioned genius, a great intellectual myth-maker, producing a regressive cosmology by setting philosophy to performing the precise function which Mr. Cowley is anxious to see the artist perform in contemporary society. "A poet or a painter does the same thing [as the engineer who says of his engine that she is cranky and affectionately pats it as if it were animate] in a richer and more communicable fashion." And the artist will also do this, if he takes Mr. Cowley seriously.

If the artist performs this function, "he gives things names and values." The weakness of such a statement appears as soon as we look at the distinction that exists between a name and a value. A name is a title describing some thing, some person, some object. A value is a property or quality inhering in a thing, a person, an object—a property that renders it useful for our purposes and our problems. When we give a name to an object we are merely labeling it. But we may not use *give* in the same sense when we come to values, because a value has some reference not merely to our own consciousness but also to the qualities, the relational potentialities, of the object itself. We cannot —even though we be poets—*give* a value to a thing. We can discover a value in it, or extract a value from it. But as soon as we begin to talk about *giving* values we become subjectivists. And the function that Mr. Cowley ascribes to art is precisely a subjectivist function.

What Mr. Cowley is doing is what many modern publicists do: they kick Idealism out on one page, and take it back to grace on the next. It is now apparent why he considers irrelevant the question of art versus propaganda. He wants art to be a game of perpetual make-believe; he wants the poet to go on forever recreating the pathetic fallacy. But this is a wish that fathers the delusion that the world is better than it is. How can such a wish be reconciled with the program that would not only *interpret* the world but also *change* it? Does such a wish make provision for that important element in literature—understanding? The answer is that it does not. It cannot act in steady sympathy with the whole trend of a literature that chooses understanding rather than myth, truth rather than comfort.

Here is the fundamental inconsistency of Mr. Cowley's critical position. Holding it, he actually banishes not only propaganda, but also any formal recognition of *art as understanding*. To say that the artist should humanize nature, that he should make life more than it is, that there is no distinction between poetry and science, between art and

171

propaganda, that art is the expression of fully assimilated beliefs—this is all one pattern, a subjective pattern that is too familiar in our literary scene. Subjectivism cuts the heart out of any attempt to formulate a critical doctrine in materialistic terms.

Mr. Cowley might contend that he does not mean these precise interpretations of his statements. All that I can reply is that, as has often been said, the road to hell is paved with good intentions. If we mean something other than what we say, we should say what we mean. And as Emerson (I believe) wrote, when an idea is let loose in the world, you can never be sure where it will land.

Again and again, revolutionary critics have told us that theory and action, word and deed, idea and object, must have a correspondence. I have, indeed, often read between their lines the implication that if one has a thought it must immediately be put into action on the nearest picket line, and that if a writer were unable to achieve this, he would prove himself to be, after all, a mere "intellectual." But, if my suspicion be correct, this is an utterly crude interpretation of the Marxian dictum that there must be correspondence between theory and action. A more intelligent interpretation would be,

I think, that our ideas and our theories must have their proper, essential, relevant reference to the things they connote in actual and objective processes in the world. And when we examine a man's statements, we must examine them by this criterion, asking what essential processes they refer to, and extending them to these essential processes in an essential manner. Ideas are not toys or playthings. They are *ideas*. Unless we are Platonists seeking a removed realm of perfected ideas, our ideas must be applied, extended, and tested in this world. Therefore, it is not what we *mean* to say that is important; it is what we *say*. It is what our communicated ideas lead to; what correspondence they have to actual processes and relationships in the world. Conceivably, Mr. Cowley may have meant to say something other than he did say. What he actually said certainly states a position; and if this position is anything else than is shown in my analysis, I should like to know what it is. Mr. Cowley's "theory" smuggles subjectivism into the critical field. It leads to looseness in making necessary distinctions. It implies that we must judge art in terms of its comfort-value. How this position can be related to a revolutionary position in criticism and literature is something I cannot

173

perceive. Mr. Cowley has described himself [73] as a "highly class-conscious petty-bourgeois critic" [74] Does this condition his subjectivist position? Or am I asking too much if I ask literary critics to talk sense, and to understand the precise meaning of the "sense" they do talk?

§ 4

When we consider some of the aims of literature, some of its concrete achievements in producing an effect upon the reader, we discover that it presents fresh insights into life, and new interpretations of its various aspects. It renders qualities and surfaces in such a way as to increase awareness and to extend sensibilities. One of the rôles of literature, aptly defined by Strachey, is that it is a reservoir for the overflow of life. The concern of literature is with life. As Chernishevski says in *Life and Esthetics*, "The essential function of art is to reproduce everything that interests man in life." [75] No one writer, whether he have a Marxist or a non-Marxist viewpoint, can deal adequately with

[73] "What the Revolutionary Movement Can Do For a Writer," in *The American Writers' Congress*, p. 65.

[74] As has been said by many a wise man, "Know thyself!"

[75] *International Literature*. I should add after "reproduce" the words *and re-create a sense of.*

everything that interests man in life. Literature as a whole, however, more or less gropes toward such an end—toward treating objective situations and conditions, representative and special predicaments of human beings, the "feeling" of locale and environment, the wide range of phenomena in life that lie outside the human consciousness, and finally, the action of this wide range of phenomena on the human consciousness. Included in this are dreams, fantasies, wishes, etc. These last do not always represent specific objective qualities existent in the objective world, but always are fragmentary copies of various specific objects or qualities, recombined in dream patterns rather than in the patterns of conscious, clear-headed cognition and apprehension.

In reproducing everything that does or can interest man in life, literature has the dual aspects mentioned at the beginning of this book: the functional and the æsthetic, the objective and the subjective. It so works on man as to create more than one impression or kind of impression. It provides him with æsthetic pleasure; reading a literary work he enjoys it for the sake of its impression upon him, because of the sensations it produces in him. Thus it is valuable to him for its own sake. This is its subjective function—presenting the individual man, in his own consciousness, with some of the goods of life, with an added sense of life, with an expanded range of experience.

Art performs other functions as well, which are not unimportant. Again to quote Chernishevski's *Life and Esthetics*.[76] "Only subject matter worthy of the attention of thoughtful man can save art from the reproach that it is the empty amusement which it only all too frequently is." In providing content, then, art serves an objective function in society. It presents material for the judgment of life and its phenomena; and along with this material it offers judgments on the material. It makes the reader more intensely conscious of the problems of life, of the predicaments of people, the possibilities and the limitations in living, the diversities in human experience, and some of the meanings, potential and actual, in this human experience. It makes value judgments on conditions, actions, thoughts, situations, environments, hopes, despairs, ideals, dreams, and fantasies.[77] It provides its audi-

[76] *International Literature*, March 6–10, 1935.

[77] The concluding proposition in Chernishevski's *Life and Esthetics* reads: "The reproduction of life is the general characteristic feature of art, its essence. Works of art often have also another purpose—to explain life. They also often express judgment on the phenomena of life."

I quote this passage because there is such general agreement with its idea. I myself did not, however, read Chernishevski until after I had drafted the argument of this book, and he is therefore not a direct

ence with additional equipment in proceeding with their own lives, and in the outward extension of their interests. It points their emotions, their impulses, their wishes, and their thoughts toward or away from certain goals. It creates, in an ideal and formal sense, the consciousness of an epoch, and is thus one of the instruments that work toward moulding and remoulding the human consciousness. Specific works of literature, worthy of attention and interest, contribute so much or so little to the re-creation of the consciousness of an epoch.

The definite meaning that I have put forward as the most adequate one for the word *propaganda* cannot logically be made to cover all the functions of literature. At this point, therefore, I suggest that in the field of literature the formula "All art is propaganda" be replaced by another: "Literature is an instrument of social influence." In doing this I am not trying to argue out of consideration the objective social functions that literature serves. Rather, I am trying to arrive at a clear-cut understanding of just what that function is, so as to

---

source of my formulation but rather an added defense of it. The statement is made not in order to prove any originality on my part, but to keep my sources clear. I am not interested in originality, but in trying to be sound and truthful. Originality in thought, anyway, does not come from any sudden great inspiration picked out of nowhere; it comes from working with what is found to be sound, and organizing and expanding that knowledge.

classify for critical purposes some of the confusions that have run rampant in revolutionary critical thought. Our concern here is not merely with what we wish literature to do, but with what we find that it can and does do. It can be propaganda—in the more limited sense of my definition of propaganda; and it can sometimes perform a function that approaches agitation. However, it often performs neither of these functions and yet does perform an objective social function. And in most cases objective social conditions themselves are such that it is only in an unimportant degree that literature serves this more limited function of propaganda, and the still more limited function of agitation.

I make these distinctions, also, not in order to preserve any high-sounding and gratuitous evaluations for art and literature. I do not defend pure æstheticism, which anyway refers to the æsthetic, subjective function of art. If an artist prefers to think that he is producing art for art's sake, there is no ground for objecting to his idea, one-sided though it may be, as long as the art he produces has content, judgment, meaning; as long as it is a reproduction or re-creation of a sense of life that is important and worthy of our attention. I am making the distinctions on the grounds of strategy and clarity, so that we may know what we are doing and what we are talking about. A leading critical confusion—as I have said—has arisen from using the word propaganda in various senses; then from hitching literature sometimes to one, sometimes to another, of these meanings; and finally from thinking that we have always had the same meanings in mind and that these meanings exhaust the rôles that literature plays objectively in society, and subjectively upon the individual consciousness of the reader. In so doing, we have produced wasted polemics; and in confronting critics who oppose Marxism, we have given them opportunities. Again and again, revolutionary criticism has led with its chin; is it any wonder that opponents have leaped in at it when such opportunities were offered?

CHAPTER XI

Growth and Decay in Literature

REVOLUTIONARY critics have frequently assured the revolutionary and proletarian writer that for subject-matter he has the whole range of history before him. Thus, Mr. Hicks has written that it is possible for the proletarian novelist to write about the past, the present, or the future, and that over this span of time there is the social area of all classes. Generally, such remarks have been just words. For while giving the world to the novelist in generalizations, critics and reviewers have taken about nine-tenths of that world back from him in specific judgments and measurements of contemporary works of literature.

Mr. Hicks, for instance, is fond of applying the phrase "Marxian insight." As I interpret this phrase, it seems to relate to the connecting up of disparate events and phenomena in economic links, a process which cuts a straight line back to the class struggle. In other words, it relates to a "Marxism" that is mechanical. The opposite tendency—revolutionary sentimentalism—has achieved a co-ordinate narrowness that binds not by the rigidity of its concepts but by the unanalyzed, roomy, and disorganized state of its crystallized emotions. Whereas the critics of one tendency speak of "Marxian" insight, those of the other revel in warning writers that they have come out of the womb of the great mother of the proletariat and must not betray that great mother. They use appeals like "responsibilities to the movement"—a phrase that is made to justify almost any and every sentimentality, deviation, and aberration so long as the proper labels are pasted on. When these two tendencies give the writer the world as his source of material, the gift is an almost empty one.

These two tendencies have, then, become the basis for drawing invidious and pernicious distinctions; they stimulate enthusiasm in the hunt for notions that fit phrases and prejudices rather than relationships and actual functions. The procedure is then productive of standards which are external to the literary process, and we are given a kind of patchwork quilt of the relevant and the irrelevant, with the latter, as likely as not, more noticeable than the former.

181

One more feature of this critical tendency should be noted here to complete the analysis. This is the devising of a more or less arithmetical scale of the social value of a work of literature in terms of whether or not it expresses hope or despair. This development results in two additional categories that cut down the center of the body or literature, dividing it into two types: the literature of growth, and the literature of disintegration—or, in other terms, the literature of "success" and the literature of "failure."

We remember Marx's statement that the seeds of the new society spring up within the shell of the old. Whitehead's *Science and the Modern World* (Macmillan) includes a description of the state of affairs in Italy during the sixth century of our era —a description which, with the change of a word or two, could be transferred to apply to the present:

"The history of the three centuries preceding the earlier period, despite the promise for the future introduced by the rise of Christianity, is overwhelmingly infected by the sense of the decline in civilization. In each generation something has been lost. As we read the records, we are haunted by the shadow of the coming barbarism. There are great men, with fine achievements in action and thought. But their total effect is merely for some short time to arrest the general decline. In the sixth century we are, so far as Italy is concerned, at the lowest point of the curve. But in that century every action is laying the foundation for the tremendous rise of the New European civilization."

If in this passage we replace *barbarism* and *Christianity* by the word Socialism, we have a striking description of the infected state of mind in our contemporary bourgeois world. It is a world haunted by anxiety. It has lost faith and certitude. Far from insisting on the "eternality" of values, it bemoans their loss and their transience. Not only because of the present social disorder and economic instability, not only because of the menace of Fascism and the virtual inevitability of war, but also because of the effects of modern scientific developments and knowledge upon men's minds and men's faiths, there is an intellectual attitude abroad describable as anxiety—an anxiety neurosis. A first stage in the intellectual self-emancipation of man is intellectual pride. So long as man has his intellectual self-confidence, he can afford a marginal surplus of scepticism, and faith—in the conventional sense of that word—is not of great meaning or necessity to him. But when he loses that intellectual self-reliance, his marginal surplus of scepticism is likely to increase even to the point of becoming a disease. This is what seems to have happened in our world, and to it may be attributed the anxiety so prevalent nowadays.

Many books reveal this anxiety as pervading the minds of numerous bourgeois intellectuals of our day. Father M. C. D'Arcy, a Jesuit intellectual whose influence in Catholic circles is growing, uses it as a starting point in his *The Nature of Belief*. He sets out to prove that belief makes men happier than disbelief, and that there are objective grounds for the establishment and proof of belief, of certitude. But in arguing along this line the author is seeking to lead men back to one of their dead gods. We recall the quondam popularity of Spengler's *Decline of the West*. The thesis of this book, which absolutizes doom as a kind of emotional prerogative and necessity, was formulated before the World War; that war only developed seeds that had been sown before August, 1914. Spengler, in exploiting the idea of doom, positing rigid cycles in connection with the idea, indulged a strong anti-intellectualist bias; and, traveling the same road farther, he enthroned irrationalism, preached Cæsarism, and turned himself into an intellectual bodyguard for the Nazi variety of Fascism.

We recall, too, the effect of T. S. Eliot's *The Waste Land* on a recent generation of poets; and the development of Eliot himself, through to *Ash Wednesday,* a poem that has many moving lines but whose mood is that of withdrawal. It completes his journey from the Waste Land to the Cross—and the cross is a gilded High Church cross. Endless similar examples could be cited, all pointing to the condition that Father D'Arcy aptly described as *anxiety.* Its wholesale spread today constrains the effectual thought of many contemporary bourgeois novelists, poets, and thinkers, often driving them into a pernicious scepticism, or else into the effort to revivify dead gods and their own dead faiths.

To tie this mood solely and one-sidedly to immediate economic forces is to risk oversimplification. Our situation in America today is not due alone to the condition of the stock market and the persistence of the depression. The break-up of contemporary society is to be seen not only in shrinking incomes; a corresponding collapse is evident in other spheres. The economic base is badly rotted; but, disintegration and decay are rushing every aspect of contemporary society: politics, religion, philosophy, literature, etc. And some have succeeded in finding a way to "glorify" this decay; they call their "glorification" of decay *Fascism.*

At the same time, we are aware of the growth

of a counter-movement—toward a social change which can only be socialism. We know, from Marx, what the basic source of this condition is, and what general directions it will take. We know that through the Russian Revolution and the establishment of the U.S.S.R. this movement has, during the last eighteen years, been given a tremendous impetus. We know that with the extension of the world revolution it will create a new Socialist Society. Socialism will slowly, gradually, permeate every sphere of human activity; will be correspondingly felt in thought, in literature, in the drama, in all the cultural spheres that compose the Socialist superstructure. But this change is not going to be brought about by fiat; it will not come merely for our wishing, nor through stout assertion that it is already here. In Russia the Revolution was a dividing line, a sharply penetrating force that cut through the heart and core of a whole nation. Soon that force was operating in all spheres of Russian life. In other countries there have been no such revolutions, and consequently these societies have not undergone any corresponding acceleration. The new culture that will grow from a new society will not precede that society, for thought and culture do not precede social changes: at best they guide toward such changes.

In view of these facts, in view of the knowledge we have now, we must realize that there are no short cuts to the solution of our current problems. We cannot, in other words, jump several relationships in our thought in order to arrive at a solution, if the conditions are not ripe for that jump. And even when we do jump stages, we must then fill in the stages we have jumped, if we are to carry forward toward further stages. We may not jump stages at random, even to arrive at a "consoling answer" to the burning needs of the hour. We actually do not know what we are talking about when we force and constrict the workings of the inter-connections between various types of phenomena, economic, material, and cultural in both the narrow and the broad sense. We only falsify when we do this; and we sow for ourselves, or for our heirs, the seeds of quite avoidable problems and despairs; we foolishly try the impossible when we seek to force historical processes beyond what the objective situations will permit. Always, a great deal of the intellectual energy of mankind must go into the correction of past errors. To be intellectually heedless, to be needlessly narrow, confined, limited, is merely to place on the shoulders of future generations the burden of correcting not only the errors that we could not have avoided but also those that we might have.

Even when a condition of social break-up prevails, there are still inter-relationships. In other words, when we present a conception of two worlds, and hierarchize them, we are in danger of oversimplifying, and thus of falsifying the picture of contemporary society; we lead ourselves off on intellectual tangents; we lose our sense of the relationships within the framework of our world. It is precisely this mistake, for instance, that destroys the validity of Robert Briffault's *Breakdown*, with its thesis that there are two worlds—one of life, and one of death. There are *not* two worlds; there is only one. That world is divided into classes. Historically speaking, despite the vicissitudes of their combats, one class is gaining ground —the proletariat; another class is losing ground— the bourgeoisie. There is a struggle between these classes, the issue involved being essentially the issue of power. Between them all sorts of lines of inter-communication cross. In dealing with these inter-connections, what we have to do is not to fulminate as Briffault does, both in *Breakdown* and in his over-rated novel, *Europa*. Our task is a far more constructive one; it is fairly described in the word *understanding*. And in the process of under-

standing, we must bear in mind that our concepts
are not ends; they are the abstractions, the "pictures" in our minds of the processes as these work
out in the raw in actual and objective situations.
Nor are they preconceptions. They are not outside
the process, but inside it. And they must be referred,
related, used in the process. Therefore, we cannot
take them outside of the process, formalize them,
lay them over the objective processes in the objective world.

But this is just what we do in bifurcating literature into a literature of growth and a literature
of decay. When we adopt simplified categories of
"success" and "failure" to prove that one type of
literature is superior to the other, we are on the
highroad to the invention of notions, to the constricting of literature, to the dissolution and confusion of its rôles in society. Our world is
characterized by twin processes, growth and decay,
which cannot be isolated one from the other and
hierarchized as two counter-standards for the appreciation of literature. Literature reflects these
twin processes, representing aspects of both; and
the greater and more detailed emphasis on one
process than on the other often depends on the
material used in any given book. The absolutized
polarization of formalized concepts of growth and

189

decay has generated much of the needless advice-mongering of critics, much of their indulgence in an empty eschatology.

On the basis of such a formalized, extra-literary, *extra-process* formula, writers are too frequently advised to give up treating material bearing on the "decay" process—material that happens to fall more truly into a pattern that, superficially regarded, seems to be a pattern of decay rather than one of success. For instance, the American novelist has often been criticized for using material in which the structure of events leads him, if he treats their implications and details honestly, to show character disintegrating, rather than integrating on a "higher" level. Sometimes it is assumed that the "bourgeois" novel has exhausted the subject of personal relationships, and that the treatment of these constitutes a step toward decadence, toward imitation of Proust and Joyce. Or it is contended that Zola said all there was to say about decay, and that the American novelist must not repeat Zola; he must write about growth, about "success." Often, in conversations with revolutionary writers, I have been told that there is a "down" literature and an "up" literature; and as we need "up" books today, we must write about—for instance—militant leaders of the sharecroppers. I do not hesitate to say that such statements merely reveal utter simple-mindedness; writers who talk thus should either get rid of such simplifications or else stop trying to write novels. For it is this brand of simplification, based on the effort to disrelate rather than relate the processes in the objective world, that has led to setting up such specious categories as, say, that of "exposure" literature.

If we accept this as a real category, what do we have? Well, first we had two kinds of literature, *bourgeois* and *proletarian*. Next there was added a third—*revolutionary*. But these three were not enough, apparently, and so a fourth was added—*exposure* literature. Then for a time it was argued that the revolutionary novelist (the novelist who has accepted the revolution) and the proletarian novelist (who has now "painfully" gained his "Marxian" insight) should abandon exposure literature. At a symposium on revolutionary writers, I heard it said that "our" writers have already reached this point: they are "done with exposure literature" and now must leave such writing to the ten millions on the bread-lines, while they themselves go on to write stories and novels that will teach the farmers how to organize, and the workers how to conduct strikes.

There is, in all such arguments, a fundamental

misconception so important that it must be pointed out. Revolutionary critics, when they advise writers in such terms, when they criticize and categorize novels in this way, are too concerned with labels and words on the one hand, and on the other with the most generalized and superficial of the impressions that are carried away from the reading of a literary work. And they ignore one of the most elemental aspects of such a work, an aspect that certainly concerns all who call themselves "Marxist" literary critics: they pay little or no heed to the *pattern* or structure of events underlying a novel or a play.

Let me take some examples. Arnold B. Armstrong's novel *Parched Earth* (Macmillan) has been, according to Granville Hicks, who rooted for it, "sharpened by the Marxian analysis of capitalism." [78] The quality of its writing and insight can be indicated by a quotation:

"Sleep had not yet thawed from her eyelids as she left bedroom for kitchen in acceptance of another day. Crossing to the gasoline range she moved on tiptoe, but small, classic feet were snubbed by two hundred pounds of corpulent body and so pressed loud squeaks and grooved dirt from the well-worn floor."

[78] *The Great Tradition*, p. 315.

The novelist has here sought to present the life
of a community in California, showing the contrasted lives of the classes and the way the class
struggle opposes them to each other. The capitalist,
who is incurably bad, has an illegitimate idiot son
by the town's whore. With considerable invention,
and with such insight and in such style as the
quotation indicates, the author leads us up to a
climax where class lines are sharpened, there to be
faced with the situation out of which the dénouement is to arise. He could not—so it has been said
in his defense—wait for the revolution to come in
the actual objective scene, nor could he truthfully
make his novel a description of the coming revolution; so he was obliged, in his passionate wish that the
revolution *should* come, to resort to symbols. The
book, therefore, on reaching its dramatic climax,
presents this symbol as an iced-on layer, in a scene
intended to be realistic. The idiot son gets some
dynamite, and—childishly liking to see things go
boom—blows up a reservoir, flooding out the entire community, hateful capitalists and all. And
this climax is accompanied by such ejaculations as
these from the idiot: " 'Boom!' he chortled with
fiendish delight." " 'Boom!' he urged." " 'Arrrh!'
he bellowed in hoarse hate of a demoniacal universe."

For a second example I may take Clifford Odets'
much discussed play, *Paradise Lost*. Michael Gold,
in a recent plea [79] that Marxian criticism be Marxian, makes these comments: *"Paradise Lost"* is a
parable of the decay of the middle class. But is the
middle class completely decadent as all this. . . .
The answer is: certainly not. . . . Odets' play is so
obviously symbolistic and not realistic that I
marvel at the rather pedestrian approach some of
the critics have taken toward it. Surely the final
speech in this play clinches the whole thesis: the
bankrupt hero accepts the bankruptcy of capitalism (in symbolic speech), and looks forward to
a new life. . . . Many of the middle class still don't
believe capitalism is finished. They hope for a
restoration of the boom days. This is the mood that
makes for Fascism. Odets tried to make them accept, emotionally, the fact that their old world is
dead. If he had done it in poetry, I think some
critics would have granted him the right to poetic
exaggeration. On the stage they demand photographic truth; reportage; labor research; the bare
exact touch; no trimmings; no transfiguration by
a wild poet's emotions."

The underlying pattern of the play is established
in the following structure of events. In the past

[79] *New Masses*, Feb. 18, 1936.

there was a paradise—before the economic crisis. In the future—when the hero brings down the curtain with a speech pinning metaphors around Engels' conception of mankind ascending from the kingdom of necessity to the kingdom of freedom —there will be another paradise. Thus dialectics, in the Marxian sense, exists as a kind of interlude, in the present when there is a crisis. But this structure of events belies Mr. Gold's contention. The play is presented both as a realistic drama and as a treatise on civilization, so that each character is set in a certain environment, and is, besides, a symbol of the doom of the middle class.

The following factors in the play suggest this doom. One capitalist is impotent. The son of another has a bad heart. His brother has sleeping sickness, and he walks around muttering symbolical statements to suggest that you don't make money on the stock market. A capitalist who represents the liberal middle class is always saying that there must be a meaning in life, and he must find it. He does find it, in a speech after all that he owns has been taken from him. A family friend is a harmless semi-idiot.

Now if we use symbols in order to represent realities, there must be some essential relation between them. My criticism of this play is that there is no *essential* relation between the symbols Mr. Odets uses and the points he seeks to establish. As a result, the play is a contrivance. Mr. Odets, in terms of a play, is arguing a case from inessential causes. If this be Marxism, then Mr. Gold may be right. I doubt it.

If we accept the definition of art that it is a reproduction and a re-creation of a sense of elements from life that interest man, we are faced with the problem of explaining just what this means. It does not mean copying, because it is useless to copy; as Chernishevski suggests so ably, nature and life in the raw are so much more rich, varied, and full, they have so much greater sensual (and, I might add, even intellectual) appeal than art, that copying is not only useless—it is phony and grotesque. Obviously, then, the reproduction of life must have some meaning. The meaning I suggest is this: the reference must be true, fundamentally, in terms of the structure or pattern of events. In other words, the connections within the work must have consistency one with the other, and this consistency must be one that is plausibly the same kind that we find in real life.

It should be emphasized that this definition does not chain literature to any obvious, peeping-through-the-keyhole kind of photographic realism.

196

For instance, *Alice in Wonderland* by Lewis Carroll fits into it, for if we examine the structure and relationships in that story we find that it presents a consistent pattern of the events in a dream or fantasy.

The application of our definition requires us to distinguish between the essential and the non-essential or less essential. If we use for our critical procedure a framework that is materialistic and monistic, if we apply the concept of process, and of dialectics to processes, we realize that every event in the world is in some way connected with every other event; that is, that the world has unity. But not every event is connected with every other event in the same way. We cannot say that every event in the universe is the cause of every other event. In all causal relationships there are *essential* causes and *non-essential* factors. Our problem, in a deterministic apprehension of the universe, is to find the essential factors and understand the way in which they are essential—the degree of their essentialness. We know that Engels (and Hegel before him) defined freedom as the recognition of necessity, and necessity means what is necessary in the development from antecedent but essential causes. The application of this concept in the realm of literary criticism and literature, then, means that within the pattern and structure of events of a literary work necessity flows out of the essential factors of environment, situation, milieu, characters—the whole complex background of relationships which is there implied and described. Symbolism in literature, following the dictates of necessity, must have essential reference to what it symbolizes, and criticism must consider literature in the light of this concept of necessity.

It is the failure of so many of our revolutionary critics to apply this concept that has resulted in the mess of irrelevancies which they have introduced into reviews, articles, and books. If we refer back to the remarks of Isidor Schneider on *The Tale of Genji* we see how irrelevant they are, in this sense. Schneider, in attempting to fix accurate points of social reference, utilized generalities so broad that they apply not only to this book, but to *all* books, as well as to many phenomena of period, culture, and locale. Again, Clifford Odets, in his *Paradise Lost*, sets out to dramatize the problems of the middle class; but his symbols contain no real necessity, and thus they make the drama internally phony. Michael Gold, in challenging this criticism of the Odets play, likewise fails to deal with essentials, and he too talks irrelevancies. Here is perhaps the most fundamental weakness in

198

nearly all revolutionary criticism so far written in America.

And it is because of this weakness, this inability to apply the concept of necessity in an essential way and with the proper references, that the element of wish-fulfillment has become so pervasive in revolutionary criticism. An example is the specious symbolism in *Parched Earth*. Wish-fulfillment results in external rather than internal conviction. Necessity is what must necessarily flow as event and implication from what has already been presented in the structure of events. If it does not flow necessarily and essentially, it represents the subjective imposition of the author's wishes onto an objective structure. This is exemplified in the cliché endings that we find in revolutionary poems, stories, novels, and plays. The curtain speech of Odets' *Paradise Lost* (Random House) betrays this element of wish-fulfillment when the character who represents the "middle class of liberal tendency" suddenly sees a light of hope which has no *essential* basis in the play itself. It comes as revelation— revelation with no sufficient previous preparation. This character then proclaims:

"No! There is more to life than this! Everything he said is true, but there is more. That was the past, but there is a future. Now we know. We dare to understand. Truly, truly, the past was a dream. But this is real! To know from this that something must be done. That is real. We searched; we were confused! But we searched, and now the search is ended. For the truth has found us. For the first time in our lives—for the first time our house has a real foundation. . . . We're not ashamed. Let them look in. . . . Everywhere now men are rising from their sleep. Men, men are understanding the bitter black total of their lives. Their whispers are growing to shouts! They become an ocean of understanding! *No man fights alone.* Oh, if you could only see with me the greatness of men. I tremble like a bride to see the time when they'll use it. My darling, we must have only one regret—that life is so short! That we must die so soon. Yes, I want to see that new world. I want to kiss all those future men and women. What is this talk of bankrupts, failures, hatred . . . they won't know what that means. Oh, yes, I tell you the whole world is for men to possess. Heartbreak and terror is not the heritage of mankind! The world is beautiful. No fruit tree wears a lock and key. Men will sing at their work, men will love. Ohhh, darling, the world is in its morning . . . and *no man fights alone!* Let us have air. . . . Open the windows."

And there are any number of such examples of wish-fulfillment in revolutionary literature. It appears, too, in criticism, where it is an even greater evil. Again and again it leads to the gen-

eralized discussion of the middle class, the proletariat, war and Fascism, the United Front, and
the Five-Year Plan, and in such a way that no essential relation is demonstrated between these
topics and the book that is being reviewed. How
often, for instance, have we not read in the *New
Masses* a book review three-quarters of which was
devoted to the reviewer's statement that the crisis
is sharpening, with a final quarter devoted to the
implication that the reviewer was a better revolutionary and a better Marxist than the author! It
is just this wish-fulfillment, growing out of a
failure to understand the concept of necessity and
the meaning of *essential* in the application of that
concept, which leads to the false bifurcation of
literature into categories of "growth" and "decay."
The meaning of growth and decay, of hope and
despair in a literary work is relative. It is easy—
a trick, in fact—to create a special emphasis proving that a book is, in such simplified terms, "up"
or "down."

In this way Malraux's *Man's Fate* can be termed
either "down" literature or "up" literature; for
on one hand it ends in the deepest tragedy, on
which the author has imposed a kind of personal
"mysticism of death"; and on the other hand its
continuous narrative impresses on the reader the

way in which a revolutionary movement lends dignity to individuals, and gives him an insight into the minds of characters who have acquired this sense of dignity from the revolutionary movement, besides conveying an idea of the sweep of that movement. By stressing one side or the other, we can prove that the book is "down" or that it is "up"—though we thereby prove our own "simplicity" as well.

In considering the structure of this novel, we find that it is true in at least one *essential* reference, in one respect relevant to the life and the events reproduced. For the real Chinese revolution did suffer a defeat; and Malraux's narrative of this revolution has therefore an essential reference to the actual revolution, and the tragic ending is explained in terms of necessity. Malraux's imposition of his "mysticism of death" cannot, I think, successfully pass the same rational test; for it is in the nature of a personal intrusion, and it has not the same element of necessity—not, at least, for me. Is this novel, then, a work of "up" literature, or of "down" literature? There is no law of logic that I know of, there are no psychological truths, that can be cited to prove that a novel of hope creates hope in the reader's mind. Hence, the whole notion of "up" literature and "down" literature is a fallacy. And

Man's Fate is only one of many novels that go to prove it.

To use categories in this way, then, and with bad logic, is to substitute labels for analysis. There is absolutely no connection between the fact that a book ends tragically and the notion that it is therefore "defeatist." Necessity is—according to my ideas—an indispensable determinant in the questions whether or not a book is to end tragically, and whether it will be what is called "up" literature or "down" literature. Any given reader's reaction of hope or of despair lies on the *subjective* side of the process. It is individual. It cannot be statistically predicted. But the pattern of events, the meanings, and the implications—the essential references of these meanings, patterns of events, and implications—all this is the *objective* side of literature. And it is the latter that constitute the most important concern of the revolutionary critic when he examines a book in order to determine its social implications. The subjective side is beyond his control. He cannot tell the reader how to feel about the book; he cannot tell the reader to be happy or sad after reading it—not even though he be "the foremost Marxist literary critic of America." But he *can*—rationally and without wish-fulfillment—tell how he interprets the objective meanings, essential references, and implications of the book. He can strive to make reading more than a mere diversion, more than a mere stimulus for evoking an "up" or a "down" feeling.

Wish-fulfillment growing out of this ignoring of the concept of necessity leads to that specious emphasis on ideology which permeates the work of our revolutionary critics. They fail to consider the actual ideological elements of a literary work in their proper light, and they fail, further, to relate its ideology to its structure of events. Prize *non-sequiturs* result. For instance, Granville Hicks' *The Great Tradition* has the following statement: "After the war men were wrestling with the problem of evil as it presented itself in concrete economic phenomena. Melville's problem was real enough, but the terms in which he stated it were irrelevant. This explains, in part, why *Moby Dick*, with all its virtues, is not comparable to the great metaphysical epics of the past, which have made room for all the principal varieties of experience in their eras. It is impossible to suppose that Melville—or anyone else living in mid-nineteenth century America—could have been a Lucretius or a Dante, and the mere fact that he could conceive of writing an epic is itself magnificent. . . . But Melville paid his price—part of which was the failure to win disciples in the following generations."

We might consider Stark Young's *So Red the Rose* (Scribner's), noting the ideology and the structure of events in this soporific novel. We discover that Stark Young here finds free play for his talents: he can reproduce the small-talk and the mannerisms of Southern aristocrats, and he can set his characters in genealogical tables so that you are constantly having to figure out whose cousin "Cud'n" Abe is. It is a novel full of enormous breakfasts, blushing belles in hoopskirts, gracefully waltzing blades and planters who talk politics and even dream in Latin. The Negroes are either "good niggers"—in the Uncle Remus pattern—or else they are bad "niggers." The white trash are *trash*. Into this atmosphere we find the Civil War bursting like a rude interruption of historical bad manners, and there follows a picture of the decay of a "gracious" civilization.

An examination of this story shows us that what Mr. Young has done is to present a formalized reverie. Instead of seeking to convey a clear sense of the ante-bellum South, he has taken facts, recorded historical memories, and the like, has sorted and resorted them until they fit not so much the patterns of "necessity" as those of reverie; thus both reader and author can wallow in melancholy memories. The net effect of Mr. Young's excursion into debilitating nostalgia is a picture of "the grandeur that was Rome" minus the real basis and the real necessities that were fundamental to that grandeur and interconnected through it. In order to paint his idealized portrait of the Old South, Mr. Young is compelled to celebrate its slave foundation. He makes this overt through one of his characters, thus: "Democracy, a good theory, a great human right, which works out none too well; slavery, a bad theory, a great human wrong, which works out none too badly."

Not all writers whose formal opinions and ideology are reactionary reveal this same harmony between their ideology and their insight and structure of events. As we draw away from third-rate novelists like Stark Young and approach the real masters of fiction, our problem is somewhat altered; we cannot dismiss the great writers so neatly. Dostoevski is a case in point. On his ideological side he was not only reactionary—he was sentimentally reactionary, sickly with his banal Christianity, his Slavophilism, his overemphasis on the necessity of the cleansing force of suffering. In *The Possessed* we find the characters again and again uttering reactionary sentiments which are obviously the author's own. Dostoevski is clearer-sighted than Stark Young, more interested in observing character accurately than he is in turning his novels into a pattern of formalized reverie, so his ideology and structure of events, his insight into human nature, and his characterizations do not harmonize with his formal ideology. If, in criticizing Dostoevski's novels, we criticize them mainly in terms of their formal ideology, we shall arrive at one estimate; while if we criticize them in terms of their structure of events, insight, and characterization, and if we draw from these their necessary and essential meanings and implications, we shall arrive at quite another estimate—an estimate that fits our definitions and criteria.

Let us take a concrete example from *The Possessed*. The futility of liberalism has never been more savagely, ruthlessly, determinedly revealed in a novel, with no sacrifice of its human features, than in Dostoevski's portrait of Stepan Trofimovitch Verhovensky. If we keep our eyes on this characterization, instead of winning an easy victory over the author's formal ideology, or imposing our own wishes and notions on him, we can appreciate its meaning. We can draw from it the implication that the liberal is futile, and that liberalism is a futile position.

How, then, are we to judge Dostoevski? Are we going to slam into his ideology, disprove it (which is easy), and then throw him into the discard? Or are we going to say that Dostoevski was all right for his time, that for his time he was or was not reactionary, that in any case he was a revolutionary in his younger days, was exiled to Siberia, and once was even on the verge of execution at the hands of a firing-squad? Or—finally—shall we recognize that his characterizations are among the most profound and incisive to be met with in any novelist?

If we adopt the first approach, we are oversimple in our extra-literary functionalism. If we adopt the second, we are stowing Dostoevski away in a museum, and attributing to his novels only the interest that we should find in any historical curiosity. Whereas, if we adopt the third approach, we are doing our real duty as literary critics—devoting ourselves to the assimilation of Dostoevski's values in and for our own time. It is this that is essentially the approach of Karl Marx in his estimate of Balzac, and of Lenin in his article on Tolstoy.

Because our age is one of social crisis, it does not —if my entire analysis be sound—follow that we must make merely a functional judgment of living literature. We know that the conditions of any age may give their own emphasis to one or the other function of literature; but this emphasis does not exhaust the values and meanings, the functions, potential and actual, of literature. One kind of emphasis on a great work does not exhaust its values and meanings. But it is just this failure to realize the existence of pluralism in literature as literature and as a part of the larger processes that go to make up society, which leads critics to make their one-sided claims.

CHAPTER XII

Conclusion

I HAVE, then, described the social rôle that living literature plays objectively in society, and I have described that rôle in the generalized formula that literature is an instrument of social influence. A function of living literature on the subjective and æsthetic side which requires at least passing acknowledgment, is its refreshment-value.[80] It might be well—for the benefit of those who defend a one-sided theory of functionalism in literature, under the banner of "Marxism"— to quote from Franz Mehring's excellent biography of Karl Marx (Covici-Friede): "He [Karl Marx] sought mental recreation and refreshment in literature and all his life it was a great consolation to him. . . . In his literary judgments he was completely free of

---

[80] An illuminating comment on the refreshment-value of art, even in times of crisis, is Maxim Gorky's anecdote of Lenin after the latter had heard some Beethoven music during the days of the Civil War. It is to be found in his *Days with Lenin*.

all political and social prejudices, as his appreciation of Shakespere and Walter Scott shows, but
he never subscribed to the idea of 'pure æstheticism', of 'art for art's sake', which is so often
coupled with political indifference or even servil-
ity." [81] As refreshment, literature can serve as a

[81] It might be suggested that many of our "leftist" critics sound less
like Marx than like Tolstoy when he began to do penance for his genius
and wrote *What Is Art?* In this book Tolstoy sacrificed all standards
and criteria of judgment, and slaughtered the great art of Europe with
a few strokes of the pen. He based his final appeal on the capacity of
the peasant. Here we find a genius throwing overboard what he can give
to society. Functional extremism leads precisely to such an end result,
and because it does it explains why so many have lost their taste on
adopting the viewpoint of "sociological," "Marxist" criticism. A writer
would not go into a factory and tell a worker how to run machinery,
unless he (the writer) happened to be an expert machinist; the reverse
should apply. The worker or the peasant, as worker or peasant, is not
the final appeal in literature either. In fact, there is no final appeal.
Literature is a matter of taste.

What the critic will do, then, if he wants to be a critic in the best
sense of the word, is to present his judgment, to try to make the work
of art understandable, and to judge its meanings and implications. His
audience is the court of final appeal only in the sense that it takes or
rejects. But one of the tasks of the critic here is that of arguing for
the acceptance of the rejection. When the critic does something else,
such as constituting the worker or the peasant as his final appeal, he
actually places his appeal in an abstraction, an abstract statement referring to the workers in the round, or the peasants in the round; because
one will find varieties of taste, understanding, temperament in the workers
or the peasants, and there will here be no unanimous agreement. Plato
is another parallel to the functional extremists: he would have banished
the poets from his Republic or subjected them to censorship. Another
parallel is the Church. Thus, John Dewey in *Art as Experience* cites the
Second Council of Nicæa in A.D. 787 as officially ordaining the following: "The substance of religious scenes is not left to the initiative of
artists; it derives from the principles laid down by the Catholic Church

relaxation from other activity, a source of pleasure to which we can resort as a temporary escape from the pressures of life. Often, in performing this function for us, it sends us back to our work with fresh stimulation, with renewed hope and energies. It provides for us what William James called "a moral holiday."

In some cases, works of living literature, although they contain truth from the viewpoint I have taken as to the concept of necessity, have principally a refreshment-value; and if we go to them it must be with that value in mind. Of such books, when we judge them great, we can say just what Marx said of Greek art. Do they not exert an enduring charm? In my estimation, one such work of literature is *Alice in Wonderland*. It might be interesting for some of our "Marxist" critics to trace back to its economic source every feature of Alice's adventures! Such a procedure would probably reveal a considerable array of information and scholarship, much of which could be related and interrelated with other human activities. I doubt, however, whether it would heighten anybody's enjoyment of *Alice*. It wouldn't heighten mine. I cannot say that it would give me a more "unified

and religious tradition. . . . The art belongs to the painter; its organization and arrangement belongs to the clergy."

esthetic experience." For in my judgment the value of *Alice* is æsthetic and subjective rather than functional and objective.

I should not take the same view of other works, such as Proust's, for instance. Here there is social reference which increases my understanding: truths about experience, personality, and social processes; ideas that tie up with social psychology and philosophy; and suggestions that are stimulating to the novelist. Thus, Proust has various kinds of objective references, and these extend my understanding; but I should not be able to present any measurement or standard of feeling and experience to prove that Proust affords me a more enjoyable experience than *Alice in Wonderland* does. And I can say the same of another work for which I have a very high respect, Maxim Gorky's *My University Days*. Its values—though different from those of *Alice*—do not militate against the values of the latter; for *Alice* serves a genuine human and literary function. There is no objective social need for establishing, say, a hierarchy showing that some other type of literary work is in a higher or a lower category; it is necessary only to establish that any given book has a genuine function as a kind of refreshment, and that there is a difference between the type with refreshment-value, such as *Alice in*

Wonderland, and the type representing a feeble escape, like *So Red the Rose.*

The living stream of literature is a process, intertwined with other processes in society. The products of this process give us understanding; they enable us to feel aspects of life more deeply; and they afford us pleasure. At various times, and according to the character of the literary output and its audience and of the society of which both are parts, one of the elements—understanding, feeling, or pleasure—may gain an ascendancy over the others; when, for instance, literature heightens our understanding and intensifies our awareness, it contributes what it is capable of toward the changing of society.

We have discussed the twin processes of growth and decay in society. A whole body, even a whole tradition, of modern literature—such as the naturalistic novel—has been instrumental in making man aware of the decay and the loss of religious belief that are so prevalent today. The rôle, here, of "exposure" literature has been utterly misunderstood. We must distinguish literature from propaganda and agitation, as I have used the words, not because of any necessary hierarchy of importance in literature, propaganda, and agitation, but because of the possibilities inherent in the function of each. No function of any of these can be said to shut the door absolutely on the rest. Literature may be propaganda, according to my definition of propaganda; but when it is, it must contain that internal consistency and that essential external reference, which I have described in applying the concept of necessity to literature.

It should be clear, now, that the effect of living literature on its reader is not the same as the effect of an advertising slogan upon a prospective customer. It cuts much deeper into the human consciousness. It cuts beneath stereotyped feelings and crystallized thoughts, furnishing the material from which extended feelings and added thought are developed. It is one of the agents serving to work out within the individual consciousness the twin processes of growth and decay in a way corresponding to the objective working-out of these processes in society. It destroys old faiths and ideals, and creates new ones, or at least lays the basis for their creation. What is important in such literature is its content, and that content is not to be taken as merely synonymous with formal ideology, generalized themes, and the explicitly stated ideas of its writers. Rather it is the shaping of life itself into literary form—a way of feeling and thinking and seeing life that the creative artist conveys to his audience—the structure of events, the quality of the characterizations, the complex impact of the work itself.

Criticism, in the literary process, should become the agent that makes for the understanding and evaluation of works of literature. It should create the atmosphere through which a maximum of value and effect, rather than a minimum, is produced by our living literature. It should strive to make the meanings of books clear, to draw out these essential meanings and refer and assimilate them in a wider social area. In performing these functions, criticism will evidently be making judgments, and on the basis of analysis; the criteria for these judgments being not alone internal to the literary process, and not alone external. Like the books to which they are applied they have both a subjective or æsthetic side and an objective or functional side. These criteria must be rationally established, tested by reference to experience, and used flexibly. In other words, they cannot be absolutized and fixed; they cannot be invented. They must have applicability to the literary work that is being judged. This is my conception of ideal criticism; and what I have tried to do in this book is to show the grounds on which it can be justified.

When literary criticism fails to play such a rôle as this, it is failing to function as it should. It is reneging on its duties and thereby sowing the seeds of confusion; for it is making no contribution toward that clarity, that lucidity, that understanding, which is rightfully asked of the critic. The critic must, as I have said, refer the book to life in an *essential* way: He must understand the book as a work of literature, reproducing elements from life, re-creating a sense of them. He must also understand the author's terms, the premises explicitly or implicitly established by the author. And this understanding cannot be merely in terms of formal ideology; it must also relate to the internal structure of events in the book. These tell the critic what the author is trying to say; they provide the clue to estimating how well, and how truthfully, the author has rendered life. The critic is thus enabled to judge the meaning of the work, both in terms of its inherent worth, and in terms of its reference to other but related meanings.

It is to be assumed, of course, that the critic has some original equipment. If he lacks original equipment in sensory capacities, in imagination, in powers of reasoning, then not all the formulæ in the world, not all the external categories he may devise, not all his academic learning, will help him.

Technique without the ability to apply it is futile. It results in formalism.

This equipment, however, can be assumed in most persons who undertake criticism. A fairly adequate power of thinking, understanding, and feeling is presumably common among them. What I challenge is the way they make use of what equipment they have—their view of the functions of literature and their procedure in measuring and legislating rather than judging it. And I am convinced that if a critic follows such a procedure— unless he seeks to judge, evaluate, relate, understand, feel, and enjoy works of living literature— his critical efforts are vain. He falls into functional extremism. He adds to the number of tasks left for others to perform in the future. He fails to advance lucidity of thinking and thus turns criticism into an instrument for confusion. Or else he sinks into impressionism, his criticism becoming totally subjective. And subjectivism leads him finally— whether he is gifted or not—into sensationalism.

We have had enough of aberrations in criticism. We have had enough extra-literary critical legislation. We have had enough blindness and sentimentalism. The health of both living literature and the revolutionary movement to which it is more and more attaching itself demands that these

218

aberrations be exposed and liquidated. It is because
of this present need that I agree with Maxim Gorky,
who writes [82]: "I do not want to give our enemies
the opportunity to laugh at us by emphasizing the
coarseness, the lack of culture and, very often, even
the ignorance of our critics. Perhaps our critics are
very well equipped ideologically, but something
seems to deter them from stating with the utmost
clarity and simplicity the science of dialectic materialism as applied to questions of art."

It is time, I think, that revolutionary criticism
should concern itself with its proper tasks, and in
a thorough and adequate way. The pious expression of generalized conclusions is insufficient. The
harping cry that criticism must be raised above
the level of personalities, the search for personal
motives rather than for ideas and criteria of judgment behind critical evaluations—such serve only
to advertise a paucity and degradation of ideas.
Critics who have ideas to express need not indulge
in pious assent to "Marxian" generalizations which
should be assimilated before one calls oneself a
"Marxist." And the factors that have militated
against our revolutionary criticism thus far have
been mechanical legislation leading to these pieties;
and sentimentalism leading to equally empty

[82] *On Guard for the Soviet Union*, p. 48.

pities. And in each case, these different tendencies either begin or end in mechanism crudity. They absolutize standards, and they absolutize Marx. For several years this process has gone on; its nature and contents have been suggested in my analysis. Its fruits in misunderstanding are incalculable. Again to quote Maxim Gorky [83]: "For many years a certain professor, writer and critic exalted mediocre writers to the height of classic authors. Serious critics paid no attention to his activities, which were hardly beneficial to the young people who heard him lecture. Now he admits that 'in the last few months he recognized some of his mistakes'! . . . A Russian proverb says: 'Words once uttered cannot be revoked'; consequently the mistakes of the professor remain."

The mistakes of our critics remain, too, and they harm the revolutionary cultural movement, which has much to assimilate, much to understand, much to produce. If it is going to assimilate what is alive from the traditions it has inherited, fight what is dead within them, and carry forward to the future, enlarging and expanding these traditions and creating new ones, it must now stop cooking up recipes for culture. It must understand, must produce culture. And to do that, it must

[83] *Ibid.*, p. 49.

liquidate its sins; it must pay now, with understanding, for the forged checks it has issued during the last few years. For it has been perpetuating old errors, and the point has now been reached where it is inexcusable to keep on doing this. For these are errors that Engels recognized years ago. I conclude with a statement from one of his letters [84]:

"Marx and I are partly to blame for the fact that younger writers sometimes lay more stress on the economic side than is due to it. We had to emphasize this main principle in opposition to our adversaries, who denied it, and we had not always the time, the place or the opportunity to allow the other elements involved in the interaction to come into their rights. But when it was a case of presenting a section of history, that is, of a practical application, the thing was different and there no error was possible. Unfortunately, however, it happens only too often that people think they have fully understood a theory and can apply it without more ado from the moment they have mastered its main principles, and those even not always correctly. And I cannot exempt many of the more recent 'Marxists' from this reproach, for the most wonderful rubbish has been produced from this quarter too."

[84] *Marx-Engels, Selected Correspondence*, No. 213, Engels to J. Bloch.